Kai Gehring

Centralization of financial regulation

A Public Choice Analysis for the European Union

Kai Gehring

Centralization of financial regulation

A Public Choice Analysis for the European Union

GRIN Verlag

Bibliografische Information der Deutschen Nationalbibliothek: Die Deutsche Bibliothek
verzeichnet diese Publikation in der Deutschen Nationalbibliografie; detaillierte bibliografische Daten sind im Internet über http://dnb.d-nb.de/ abrufbar.

1. Auflage 2010
Copyright © 2010 GRIN Verlag
http://www.grin.com/
Druck und Bindung: Books on Demand GmbH, Norderstedt Germany
ISBN 978-3-640-81114-4

Seminar HS 2010:

"The Economics of International Organizations"

Does Centralization improve regulation -
A Public Choice analysis for the European Union

Seminar paper

Chair of Economics, esp. Political Economics

University of Mannheim

Fall term 2010

by

cand. rer. oec. Kai Gehring

I. Table of Contents

II. List of abbreviations and definitions

AB = Assessment Base

De Larosière Group = A group of economists chaired by Jacques de Larosière that was set up by EC President José Manuel Barroso and contained European economists.

EBA = Proposed European Banking Authority

ECA = European Court of Auditors

EC = European Commission

ECB = European Central Bank

ECOFIN = The Economic and Financial Affairs Council (ECOFIN) is composed of the Economics and Finance Ministers of the 27 European Union member states

EIA = Proposed European Insurance Authority

EP = European Parliament

ESA = Proposed European Securities Authority

ESRC = Proposed European Systemic risk Council

EU = European Union

EU Council = Institution that represent the national member states in the EU

EU Court = The European Court of Justice (officially the Court of Justice), is the highest court in the European Union in matters of European Union law

FED = The Federal reserve system is the central banking system of the United States. Its most important board is the presidentially appointed Federal Reserve Board. Regards itself as an independent entity within government

FSF = Financial Stability Board, a forum to promote financial stability, founded by the G7 group

GSE = Government Sponsored Enterprise

Group G30 = An international body of leading financiers and academics which aims to deepen understanding of economic and financial issues and to examine consequences of decisions made in the public and private sectors.

G30 reform = A report outlining patters for regulatory reform chaired by Paul A. Volcker

MEP = Representative in EP

MBS = Mortgage-backed securities

Public agents = European and National politicians and bureaucrats

Subsidiarity = An organizing principle that calls for matters to be handled by the smallest, lowest or least centralized competent authority.

III. List of figures

IV. List of tables

Figures and tables in Appendix:

Tables:

Table 4: Current studies on the effects of decentralization (p.34 -36)

Table 5: Overview of variables for the 27 EU Countries – Highest and lowest highlighted (p.37-38)

Table 6: Voting rights in EU Council (p.39)

Table 7: Calculation of Council decisions due to the three majority criteria (p.40)

Figures:

Figure 6: Geographical overview of preferences for European or National level (p.41)

Figure 7: Geographical overview of preferences for supervision or transparency (p.42)

1. Introduction

Financial regulation has played an unfavorable role in the financial crisis. Many reform proposals conclude from its failure that there is a need for more and tougher rules (Group30 2009). Consolidating existing regulatory bodies and a centralization of authorities seem to be the ubiquitous answer of many politicians[1]. In the European Union (EU), a reform proposal has gained support by the European parliament (EP) and the European Commission (EC), which would mean additional competences and staff for European bureaucracies. Because it would centralize large parts of regulation and supervision, political arguments focus on the allocation of competences and power[2]. However, it is not sure if the proposed changes would have any effect in preventing future crises.

The structure of this paper follows a systematic approach to demonstrate problems with this proposal. At first, I show in chapter 2 that the role of regulation and governments in the financial crisis is ambiguous. What is viewed as market failure was sometimes only a rational response to incentives set by regulation. It is often stated that markets did not work efficiently, and the obvious solution is to rely on governments and regulators to fix the problems. I check if international comparison provides support for consolidating regulatory bodies. In Chapter 3, I assess in detail the proposed EU reform that focuses on establishing new bureaucracies and implementing more rules. I will use a structured Public Choice approach to evaluate the reform proposal and assess special interests of involved political parties. Chapter 4 examines the role of the EU **Council** and voter preferences. Considerable power in the EU decision-making process rests with parties that support centralization and more regulation. With various approaches, it is tried to shed light on the position of the **Council** as the representation of member states. While European institutions might embrace additional power and competences, rational voters in the member states should oppose harmful, excessive regulation and centralization. However, a detailed analysis of government and voter preferences reveals that both are likely to have biased preferences in favor of too much regulation.

Decentralization and political competition might be the only way to prevent overregulation, which will constraint future growth. With this in mind, the obvious solution of more regulation, relying on bureaucracies and omnipotent governments, seems less advantageous. Moral hazard problems and misleading incentives, and inefficient capital requirements could be the real problem, not the quantity of market rules. Transparency and public disclosure of information might be superior to relying on some "competent authority" [3] that single-handedly prevents future crises.

Reforms should be judged by their efficiency; they should neither follow the interest of the banking lobby, nor exploit voter ignorance to expand political power and influence.

---

[1] http://www.europarl.europa.eu/sides/getDoc.do?pubRef=-//EP//TEXT+REPORT+A7-2010-0205+0+DOC+XML+V0//EN
[2] http://www.euractiv.de/finanzplatz-europa/artikel/klinz-fdp-staaten-mssen-scheinheiligkeit-aufgeben-003336,
http://www.spiegel.de/wirtschaft/unternehmen/0,1518,713847,00.html
[3] http://www.europarl.europa.eu/news/expert/infopress_page/042-77983-186-07-28-907-20100706IPR77978-05-07-2010-2010-false/default_de.htm

2. Financial Regulation

Regulation and supervision has been at the heart of criticism after the recent financial and economic crisis. Several reform proposals have been made to "avoid" the next crises, which mostly focus on international cooperation and expanding the influence and power of regulatory agencies (Group30 2009; The De Larosière Group 2009). Slow progress with reforms is often blamed on the strong influence of the banking lobby, political self-interest or the international unwillingness to cooperate[4]. Thus, as all these problems involve collective decision-making, they can only be fully understood by adding a public choice perspective (Gadinis 2008). Developing optimal ideas of future regulation will not make much sense if political summits fail to implement the ideas. Disregarding the political level of the discussion will make unhelpful, but popular new regulations more probable.

In this chapter, I start with shortly outlining the role and types of regulation. I will structure and evaluate arguments concerning the desirability of competing systems, and try to exemplify what I call the dilemma of regulation. It is not possible to construct a perfect regulatory framework, and very often well-meant attempts can cause adverse effects. This can be seen in the ambiguous role of politics and regulation played in the financial crisis. A comparison of national systems with one or multiple regulatory bodies suggests that besides the discussion about centralization and fusion of supervisory bodies, organizational structure has only a minor influence on efficiency.

2. 1. Kinds of regulation

Financial regulation can be broadly divided into safety-and-soundness regulation and compliance. Safety-and-soundness regulation's fundamental purpose is to protect fixed-amount creditors from losing their funds, and to provide stability within the financial system. This is of central interest for this paper. Compliance regulation should protect individuals from unfair treatment and misleading advice[5]. A compliance issue in the crisis was "misstating and omitting key facts about a financial product tied to subprime mortgages"[6] through Goldman Sachs. They have been sued by the US Government and private investors for this potentially criminal act. However, this is mainly a topic for criminologist and lawyers. When I use the term regulation, it encompasses the setting of rules and their supervision. Where necessary I will further discriminate between both. Instead of going into excessive details of single regulations, I rather try to portray the big picture.

2. 2. Regulatory competition

Whereas for instance in the area of accounting significant international harmonization has been achieved, "countries financial laws remain characteristically heterogeneous" (Gadinis 2008, p.449). Sinn (2003a; 2003b) has repeatedly brought up arguments against this kind of policy competition. He argues that governments have imposed regulation to correct market failures due to asymmetric

---

4 http://www.spiegel.de/wirtschaft/unternehmen/0,1518,658139,00.html
5 http://www.econlib.org/library/Enc/FinancialRegulation.html
6 http://www.sec.gov/news/press/2010/2010-59.htm

information and limited liability. This regulation has positive international policy externalities. "Systems competition" might however re-instate the initial market failure and lead to a **race-to-the-bottom**. However, empirical studies show that international competition can also trigger a **"race-to-the-top"** (Vaubel 2008a), and that there is a positive effect of policy competition on innovation (Bernholz and Vaubel 2004). Consequently, others have rejected Sinn's claims, and expressed a more positive view (Baltensperger 2003). I will treat benefits of centralization and consolidation in more detail later.

2. 3. The dilemma of regulation

It is very easy for an economist to identify a problem, describe its causes and conclude that regulation should fix it. However, in the real life it seems like this is not the full story. Politicians and interest groups can try to misuse regulation to extract rents (Brennan and Buchanan 1984). This can lead to excessive and harmful regulation. There are other caveats of more and centralized regulation. As with all government failure, the problem is not primarily that regulators are either incompetent or lack knowledge. However, they have to work in an area of contradictory and conflicting interests. Stigler implied that "...as a rule, regulation is acquired by the industry and is designed and operated primarily for its benefits" (Stigler 1971, p.3). Yandle concluded that regulation is often required "...as protection from competition, from technological change, and from losses that threaten profits and jobs" (Yandle 1983, p.13). Political representatives often push for exceptions for certain branches or companies that are situated in their constituency[7]. This does not imply that regulation is always a bad thing, but it does add additional complexity.

Problems with this **regulatory capture** have been classified in three categories: **Interest group theories, Tollbooth theories** and **Principal-Agent Theories** (Boehm 2007). **Interest group theories** focus on the influence of lobby groups on regulators and the costs of rent seeking activities, with a passive role of public agents. **Tollbooth theories** point to the possibility of public agents actively extracting rents from regulated industries through bribes and campaign contributions. Asymmetric information is the core of **Principal-Agent theories**. The fact that "firms have private information that is hard for citizens or their representatives to obtain" (Bó 2006) is indeed an issue that is hard to overcome.

Even if regulators only pursue the public interest, regulation can only be static while company behavior is dynamic.[8] A reason for failing regulation is that the regulated circumvent it by changing their behavior. Offsetting behavior will counter the intended effects of regulation (Peltzman 2010). The **"Peltzman effect"** describes people reacting to a safety regulation by increasing other risky behavior. It is in the nature of markets to find a way to implement the most efficient solution. If this

---

[7] E.g. Companies with especially high energy consumption have been exempted from the European Union Emission Trading Scheme - http://de.wikipedia.org/wiki/EU-Emissionshandel
[8] http://jagouldworld.blogspot.com/2010/03/allan-meltzer-market-failure-or_18.html

is to avoid regulation, it is often called **regulatory arbitrage**[9]. A popular answer has been to implement more and stricter rules. Regarding financial regulation, the public expectation for new regulation is no less than to prevent the next crisis. However, can governments and regulation really be expected to help?

2. 4. The role of regulation in the recent financial crisis

2.4.1. Regulation, incentives and amplifying effects

Subjectivism cannot completely be avoided in an analysis of the financial crisis, and it is impossible to incorporate all aspects. Hellwig (2009) provides a coherent analysis of the crisis. The main points I want to outline are the adverse effects of often well-meant, but economically unsound policies and rules. U.S. policy, mostly through government-sponsored enterprises (GSE) like **Freddie Mac** and **Fannie Mae,** encouraged the provision of long-term variable-interest loans to certain groups[10]. Long before the crisis, studies concluded that "there is an inherent conflict between the GSE's status (…) and the government mission they are expected to perform" (Wallison and Ely 2000, p.6). While the risk of the massive expansion of these GSE's has not gone unnoticed[11], the measure to spread mortgage risk worldwide was widely accepted in both academics and politics[12]. Even in the retrospective, "in principle, the securitization of such risks should be regarded as a good idea" (Hellwig 2009, p.134). This is why once the U.S. mortgage holders started to default, losses occurred at banks worldwide. There were three main factors in the run-up to the crisis I want to highlight.

The first is that politics interfered in the housing market and created an unstable equilibrium in the mortgage market. In the end, markets proved the impossibility of providing mortgages to people who cannot afford them. The second is, that it was a reaction to the U.S. Standards& Loans crisis in the 1980s that regulators and academics pushed for allowing commercial banks to invest in riskier assets, including MBS (Brumbaugh Jr and Litan 1989). While the actual effect of a "too-big-too-fail"-bank going bankrupt are debatable, the fear of it has prompted politicians and central banks to rescue these banks. The prospect to be bailed out provides wrong incentives for banks and leads to adverse effects. Obviously, if there is a reduced risk of going bankrupt, the tendency to endeavor in risky behavior increases. Overall, it does at least increase the number of banks that will be difficult to liquidate.

The third factor is that capital requirements were too low, too complicated and misleading (Vaubel 2010). The risk-adjusted capital requirements in Basel guidelines allowed banks to under-

---

9 Goldman Sachs plans already how to circumvent new regulation before its implementation, http://ftalphaville.ft.com/blog/2010/08/02/303751/overcoming-the-volcker-rule-with-etfs/
10 "(…)to support the housing industry(…)on of its solutions was to encourage the use of new types of mortgage instruments. They (US government) have revised their charter and operate to increase the availability and affordability of homeownership for low- moderate- and middle-income homebuyers (Fabozzi 2001, p.6)
11 "The lower interest rates (…) permit them to out-compete any private-sector rival and dominate any market. (…) their dominance of the mortgage market grows ever greater (Wallison and Ely 2000, p.2-3)
12Support for example "Our results are quite intuitive and demonstrate the benefits of geographic diversification" (Calem and La Cour-Little 2004, p.671), "We conclude that geographic diversification is an important mortgage portfolio objective (Corgel and Gay 1987, p.256), also (Mueller and Ziering 1992), (Ogden, Rangan, and Stanley 1989)

capitalize using regulatory gaps (Hellwig 2010). Market actors did rely on models using ratings and backward-looking data that were providing a misleading sense of security. Regulation encouraged and set incentives to buy MBS securities[13]. Not only were low-income households taking on unsustainable loans, but also the government quasi-guarantee lured private investors in the market[14]. Regulators and Supervisors failed to prevent banks from exploiting regulatory gaps. Once U.S. mortgage holders started to default, losses occurred at banks worldwide. Resolving **Fannie Mae** and **Freddie Mac** will costs U.S. taxpayers up to $400 billion, more than for all other failed American banks together. Misleading incentives or error rather than limited liability of managers and "sheer greed" of bankers are the most obvious reasons (Hellwig 2009; Vaubel 2009).

In addition to these factors, several **amplifying effects** played a role in augmenting the crisis (not in causing it). Market participants took part in deals that they knew to be unsound, because markets closely resembled what Keynes had called a "beauty contest"[15]. "Irrational exuberance", "animal spirits" and "behavioral cascades" contributed to the widespread panic in the markets (Akerlof and Shiller 2010; Gintis 2009). The **Interbank lending market** collapsed because of newly introduced uncertainty in the market. **Amplifying effects** of the crisis can be seen as **market failure**.

2. 5. Consolidation

2.5.1. Regulatory approaches

Among the most common themes in reform proposals is the wish for consolidation in the "alphabet soup"[16] of regulatory agencies. It is obvious that a lack of consolidation was at least not the only reason for failed regulation. (Fresh and Baily 2009) have structured regulatory approaches In three categories. The **Integrated approach** involves a single regulator overseeing all financial institutions and providing all kind of regulation. If safety-and-soundness and compliance regulation are separate it can be referred to as the **Twin Peak approach**. The **Functional approach** implies that institutions are supervised based on type of business. Challenges lie in the coordination between the functional regulators. Under the **Institutional approach,** the legal status of an institution defines its supervisor. It is less flexible, as institutions can seek regulatory arbitrage through changing their legal status and picking their most convenient regulator.

---

[13] 1984 the government passed the Secondary Mortgage Market Enhancement Act (SMMEA) to improve marketability of MBS, The Financial Institutions Reform, Recovery and Enforcement Act 1989 (FIRREA) encouraged loan origination, The Tax Reform Act 1986 allowed the creation tax-free special purpose vehicles.
[14] " If you are tired of of trying to outguess the stock market, consider MBS with their high yields and above average safety" Your Finances, 75 A.B.A. J. 108 (1989) Mortgage-Backed Securities; Dunnan, Nancy
[15] On a meeting with investment bankers from Lehmann Brothers that I attended, they remarked that they would participate in the MPTS trading as long as everyone else does so, because there seems to still be money to earn.
[16] http://www.finreg21.com/lombard-street/spelling-regulatory-reform-restructuring-our-alphabet-soup-financial-regulators

2.5.2. International comparison

Country	Regulatory approach	Notes
Canada	Twin Peak	Large role for provincial regulation
US	Functional	Includes Institutional aspects
UK	Integrated approach	Principles based
Australia	Twin peak approach	Long and systematic reform process
France	Functional approach	CB involved, "three peaks"
Germany	Integrated approach	Overlapping competences
Hong Kong	Institutional approach	Functional elements
Japan	Integrated approach	Politics strongly involved
Netherlands	Twin peak approach	CB as prudential regulator
Spain	Functional	Changing to twin peak
Switzerland	Functional	Changing to integrated

Table 1 - International comparison of regulatory approaches

Table 1 provides an overview of differences between international regulatory approaches[17]. It is not the purpose of this table to explore in depth country characteristics, but to extract the relevant conclusions. It can be seen that regulatory systems vary broadly across nations, but there seems to be a trend towards the **Twin Peak** or **Integrated approach**. However, there seems to be no clear pattern for a preferred, "first-best", regulatory approach. Two countries that have mastered the crises quite successfully, and often ascribe that to their regulatory structure, are Canada and Australia. Both broadly adopted a Twin Peak approach. However, this is where the similarities stop.

The Canadian system has strong role for the federal states, although this is otherwise often blamed for inefficient regulatory competition. The Australian system is strongly based on principle-based regulation, which focuses more on outcomes than on rules. This involves intensive dialogue between regulators and regulated institutions, which on the other hand could be criticized as opening a gateway for lobbyists. The Australian example seems to favor principle-based regulation[18]. However, the UK had implemented this approach some years before the crisis, and was among the countries most severely affected. The overview suggests that there is not a single best regulatory approach. If countries adopt a Twin Peak or integrated approach seems not to affect regulatory outcomes as much as sound principles and effective coordination. It is possible that the same problems continue to exist with an **Integrated** or **Twin-peak approach**, only now within on organization instead of between different institutions. The functional and institutional approach might be problematic when business changes their field of business or their legal form quickly.

---

[17] http://www.finreg21.com/lombard-street/what-does-international-experience-tell-us-about-regulatory-consolidation
[18] http://www.treasury.qld.gov.au/office/knowledge/docs/financial-accountability-handbook/1-3-principles-based-legislation.pdf

France has relied on a more functional approach, with three authorities responsible for different business types and a large role the Central Bank. The country was among the ones most severely hit by the crisis.

Empirically, a comparison of regulatory structures in 150 countries by Barth, Caprio, and Levine (2006) concludes that private monitoring is most important for supervision efficiency. Very often, blind faith into regulators is not justified more than waiting in "till angels govern". It fails to find a relation between regulatory structures or power of supervisors and the performance of the banking system. On the contrary, more government monitoring seems to "crowd out" (more efficient) private monitoring, because it leads to a false sense of security. In many cases, corruption, lobbyism and incompetency undermine even the most sophisticated regulatory approaches.

3. Centralizing regulation and supervision in Europe

Chapter II has highlighted the shortcomings and role of regulation in the crisis. Different regulatory approaches in various countries have not been clearly related to country performance in the crisis. Nonetheless, consolidation, merging existing agencies and introducing more rules are often viewed as the best solution to prevent future crises and are part of reform proposals for the EU. Subsequently, I will examine reform proposals and evaluate them using a structured framework. It considers the role of Subsidiarity, varying interests and decision-making rules.

3. 1. EU institutions and positions

3.1.1. Subsidiarity in the EU treaties

Subsidiarity has always been a guiding principle for the European Union. The Single European Act (1986) stated, "The central authority should only act (...), if it achieves targets better than national governments would" (Ischia 2004, p.68). Since the Treaty on European Union (Maastricht 1993), it is officially established in European Law. The Treaty of Lisbon (2009) allows national parliaments to force the EC to review proposals, if they are considered incompatible with Subsidiarity. The official glossary of the European Union states that "decisions are taken as closely as possible to the citizen and that constant checks are made as to whether action at Community level is justified in the light of the possibilities available at national, regional or local level. (...)"[19] The actual enforcement of Subsidiarity is more complicated. On several issues, the EC has used loopholes in the treaties to centralize and enhance its influence (Ischia 2004). The preamble of the Lisbon treaty does mention "the process of creating an ever closer union (...) in accordance with the principle of Subsidiarity". However, Subsidiarity is not complementary to an "ever closer union". On the contrary, it implies a detailed cost-benefit analysis before centralizing any individual policy field.

---

[19] http://europa.eu/scadplus/glossary/subsidiarity_en.htm

3.1.2. Interests for centralization

Sometimes it is assumed that the primary objectives for European and National governments and bureaucracies are to expand their power. This is too simple. Other motives also have to be regarded in this framework. Figure 1 shows the most important institutions regarding centralization in Europe.

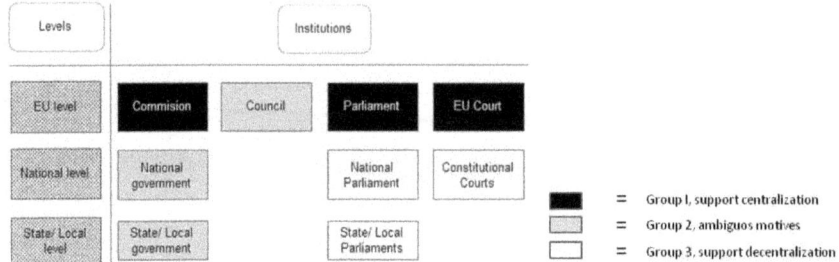

Figure 1 - Interests of actors in EU decision-making processes

Group I consists of the **EC**, the **EP**, and the **EU Court**. They all clearly support further centralization. The commission[20] regards itself as the "guardian of the treaties", the parliament mainly consists of convinced Europeans, and the **EU Court** is often called an "engine of integration". Vaubel (2008; 1996) has shown that constitutional courts have an interest and play a significant role in enhancing centralization within a country. None of this does imply that these institutions do merely want to increase their power. People could also really be convinced that centralization is the right way to overcome problems. Through self-selection, these people are more likely to work in these institutions. Group II are the **EU Council**, National and State/local **parliaments**. They have a clear interest in preserving their competences. National Constitutional Courts have often (unsuccessfully) ruled against centralizing legislation. The incentives for group III, the National and State/local **governments** are ambiguous. While they are likely to want to preserve their status, the delegation of unpleasant tasks to the EU has more than once been an easy way to avoid voters' displeasure (Vaubel 2006; 1994). Whether a decision is made by real conviction or to increase power is not clearly distinguishable. The aims to help the public interest and the wish for an "ever-closer" EU often go along. Nonetheless, even good motives do not guarantee good results.

3.1.3. Reform Proposals for the EU

One of the most prominent reform proposals was the G30 project on financial reform chaired by Paul A. Volcker (Group30 2009). The proposal focuses on **additional, consolidated supervision, more regulation**, the **central bank supervising financial stability**, the **independence of regulatory institutions**, and somehow a better **international coordination**. The proposals exhibit wide skepticism about markets; the unfortunate role of the U.S. government, the FED, and Freddie Mac and Fannie Mae on the other hand is only shortly mentioned. A similar report focused on the EU has

---

[20] It should be remembered that the commission are not only 27 commissioners, but also the associated bureaucracy consisting of about 20.000 EU public agents.

been prepared by the so-called "High level group", chaired by Jacques de Larosière[21]. It does not further analyze the causes for **government failure**. The role of **international trade imbalances** and **artificially low central bank rates** is mentioned, merging of commercial and investment banks has made the world "a more complex" (The De Larosière Group (DLG) 2009, p.62) place. The actual reform proposals consist mainly of **more, stricter** and **consolidated regulation**. Interestingly, it does explicitly highlight the **EU** interest for raising rival's costs. "The **EU** has a clear interest in promoting worldwide consistency of regulatory standards towards the high level benchmarks" (DLG 2009, p.60).

Anyhow, the report does mention the need for better information exchange, and a way to handle and a possible liquidation of distressed banks. In rare honesty, it admits that, "it is inevitable that there will be failures (in regulation) from time to time" (DLG 2009, p.39). This does not stop the proposal from mainly relying on regulators to anticipate and prevent future crises. At the core of the proposal are two reforms: At first, "the Financial Stability Forum (FSF) , (…), is put in charge of promoting the convergence of international financial regulation to the highest level benchmarks" (DLG 2009, p.61). Secondly, a European System of Financial Supervision (ESFS) and a European Systemic Risk Council (ESRC) should be installed in two stages.

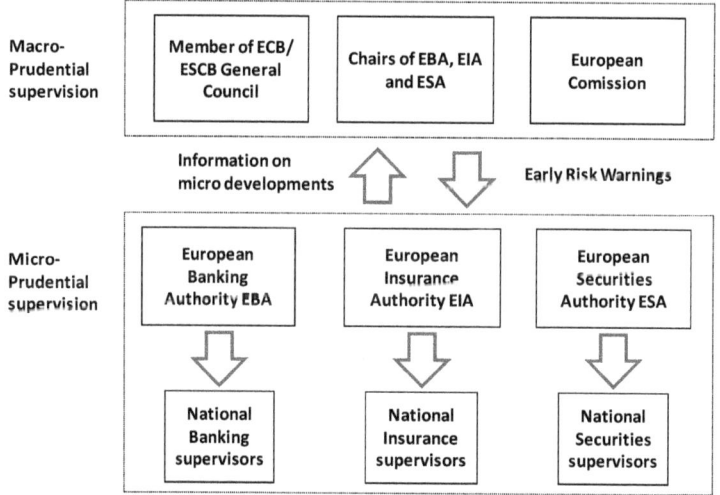

Figure 2 - Proposed Structure for EU regulation and supervision, compare (The De Larosière Group 2009, p.57)

At the key of the target structure is a new committee to oversee the "systemic-effects" of regulation, the **ESRC**. It cooperates with three new authorities: a **European Banking Authority (EBA)**, a **European Insurance Authority (EIA)** and a **European Securities Authority (ESA)**. These authorities are extensions of three existing committees. The three authorities "should be managed by (…) the chairs of the national supervisory authorities. The chairpersons and director generals (...) should be full-time independent professionals (...) (author note: "appointed") by the **EC**, the **EP** and the **Council** (...) for a period of 8 years "(DLG 2009, p.55). The most important additional competencies are legally binding mediation between national supervisors; the adoption of binding supervisory standards, and licensing and supervision of specific EU-wide institutions (e.g. Credit Rating Agencies). The role of national authorities would mainly diminish to executing central orders and being "responsible for the day-to-day supervision of firms" (DLG 2009, p.56).

The main effect of the **ESRC** is that the **ECB** would officially add financial stability to its targets. In addition, the role of the **EC** would increase the political influence on regulation. The French system was described earlier. It is strange that its structure closely resembles the proposed one. The performance of the French system in the crisis was not particularly outstanding. However, the **European Commission** has mainly welcomed the propositions. [22], major changes are the proposed names of authorities[23]. The **EC** proposes the **ESRC** to be established through **Article 95 of the EC Treaty**. Voting rights in this board (simple majority voting) would be given to "the Governors of national central banks; the President and the vice-President of the **ECB**; a Member of the **EC**; the Chairpersons of the three European Supervisory Authorities". The Board can supposedly act against the interest of individual member states, as these" may not always coincide with (...) maintaining financial stability in the European Union as a whole." Two consultation rounds with involved parties have highlighted worries about the allocation of power in the proposal[24]. The new institution shall "take the measures necessary for the protection of the confidential nature of the warnings" which would lead to less instead of more openness.

The **EP** has further added **strict supervision** and **regulation** of private sector remuneration systems to the **EC** propositions[25], including data about individual managers' salaries. This would shift considerable power and influence to the **MEP**'s. Throughout the text, most difficult actions are delegated to "competent authorities". Why these authorities should have superior knowledge to other market participants is spared together with other complicated details. [26] The main representative organ of the member states on this issue is the **Economic and Financial Affairs Council (ECOFIN)**. In its statement it signals, "Agreement on the substance", so that the new authorities "can be operational from 1 January 2011"[27]. The authorities would receive power to ensure "harmonized rules" and a "common regulatory culture". In general, the **Council** gives priority to enhancing cooperation opposed to new central authorities[28].

---

[22] http://eur-lex.europa.eu/LexUriServ/LexUriServ.do?uri=COM:2009:0252:FIN:EN:HTML
[23] http://ec.europa.eu/internal_market/finances/committees/index_en.htm
[24] http://ec.europa.eu/internal_market/consultations/docs/2009/fin_supervision/summary_en.pdf;
http://ec.europa.eu/internal_market/consultations/docs/2009/fin_supervision_may/replies_su mmary_en.pdf
[25] http://www.europarl.europa.eu/sides/getDoc.do?pubRef=-//EP//TEXT+REPORT+A7-2010-0205+0+DOC+XML+V0//EN
[26] An important amendment is that a "delegation of power (...) may be revoked at any time by the European Parliament or by the Council".
[27] http://www.consilium.europa.eu/uedocs/cms_data/docs/pressdata/en/ecofin/115787.pdf
[28] http://register.consilium.europa.eu/pdf/en/09/st14/st14239.en09.pdf

3. 2. Public Choice Analysis

The proposals would mean a considerable shift of power and competencies from the member states to the **EU**. Common sense suggests that banks that operate on a European or worldwide scale should be supervised through a worldwide authority. Common rules should ensure a level playing field for all competitors. It has been shown that very often, the unintended effects of rules countervail against the (well-meant) intended effects. In the economic literature, centralizing political power was at first treated by the "First-Generation Theory of Fiscal Federalism" (Oates 2005, p.350). It was mainly concerned with the "assignment of functions to the different levels of government" (Oates 2005, p.352); maintaining the assumption of a benevolent government. The role of economists was mainly to determine market failures and let government agencies fix the failures. **Public Choice** literature brought the most important extension to this field by including the possibility of government failure (Frey 2009; Tullock 1967; Buchanan and Tullock 1962). The approach improved the consistency in economic analysis by assuming that all individuals maximize their own utility. Goals of public agents have be modeled as maximizing the size of their budget (Niskanen 1971), maximizing revenues that the public sector extracts from the economy (Brennan and Buchanan 1980), the chance of (re-) election (Artés and Viñuela 2007; Dreher and Vaubel 2004, Seabright 1996) , and higher salaries and bigger staff (Vaubel 2006; Vaubel 1996).

Misperceptions about political processes do exist in both the public and parts of economics. Not including **Public Choice** aspects will always lead to an incomplete analysis of any subject that involves collective decision-making. In the following, I rely on a framework by Ederveen, Gelauff, and Pelkmans (2008a), to provide a structured analysis of the problem of centralizing regulation. Table 2 provides a broad overview of the revised framework.

	Decentralization	Centralization
Policy uniformity	- Preference matching - Transaction costs	- Internalize Externalities - Economies of scale
Leviathan	- Accountability - Political-competition - Limit bureaucracy	- Prevent race-to-the-bottom - Supervision
Lobbying	- Reduce impact of homogenous interest groups	- Reduce impact of heterogeneous interest groups
Policy learning	- Yardstick competition, - Implementing best practice	
Complementarities	- Limit bureacracy	- Expanding bureaucracy
Decision making	- Decision-making costs - Less logrolling	- External costs - Raising rival's costs - Conflicts of interest

Table 2 - Structured approach to assess benefits of centralization

3.2.1. Policy uniformity

Preference matching

Even if governments maximize the welfare of their constituencies, problems with centralization can arise. A central government will most likely pursue a uniform policy in all jurisdictions, as it is politically very difficult to provide different amounts of a public good in different locations (Oates 2005). If information is costly, the local governments will have superior information of local circumstances. De Tocqueville wrote that centralized "legislation cannot adapt itself to the exigencies and the customs of the population, which is a great cause of trouble and misery" (Tocqueville 1863, p.163). Oates' (1972) de-centralization theorem states, that decentralization can always increase welfare if differences in preferences exist.

Preferences about financial regulation vary strongly across European Countries. Survey results that I show in more detail later confirm these. Problems occur for rules and supervision. The Basel requirements are an example for the attempt to establish common regulation. Differing preferences and conflicts are exemplified by the discussion between largely equity-dependent American companies and European companies that rely more on debt. A common (worldwide) supervision would in addition significantly suffer from information constraints. The sheer amount of computing and intellectual capacity required is enormous. While common rules could still rely on the market to process information, supervision requires an agency to solely cope with that. Overwhelming evidence indicates the superiority of groups and markets over central agencies in decision-making (Surowiecki 2004).

Externalities

Policy decisions of one state can lead to positive or negative externalities in other states. By forming bigger groups or through centralization, the internalization of externalities is theoretically possible. Central government can try to compensate or penalize local governments to achieve a pareto-superior outcome (Oates 2005). A regulation level that is too low in one country may cause external effects in other countries. Failing banks in one country might damage the reputation of banks everywhere. Therefore, it is one target of regulators to maintain market confidence.[29] Common regulation like Basel II can cause external effects. If one bank suffers credit losses and losses part of their equity capital, it is forced to reduce lending, including lending to other banks. This partly caused the process that led to the breakdown of the interbank lending-market. Very often advocates of centralization merely point to the costs of externalities and assume that the problem will be solved. However, the practical implementation always lags behind the theoretical optimum. Assessing externalities and implementing correction measures is always extremely difficult and not necessarily better than the original result.

---

[29] http://www.staff.city.ac.uk/p.booth/regulationstudents1.pdf

Economies of scale

There is no perfect organizational structure for regulation authorities, as the real efficiency problem is one of governance structure. In essence, integrating national regulators into a common European organization means vertical integration. Increasing size and centralization in organizations are limited due to "limitations on gathering, processing and communicating information" (Macher and Richman 2008, p.3). An optimal organizational structure should lead to a "transaction-cost-economizing result" (Williamson 2005, p.6). While integration might save some costs due to avoiding a duplication of tasks and scale effects, it also increases transaction costs. European countries are still very heterogeneous. Keeping in mind unavoidable problems with different languages, varying legal systems, cultural backgrounds, and differing objectives we can assume that transaction costs in a common EU authority would be substantial. In Transaction-cost economics, a system that consists of market and hierarchical elements is called "hybrid". Such a system that enhances coordination between national regulators, but does avoid new big bureaucracy and high transaction costs could be a more efficient alternative (Table 3). Improving salaries and providing clear political objectives could improve operational efficiency more than consolidation.

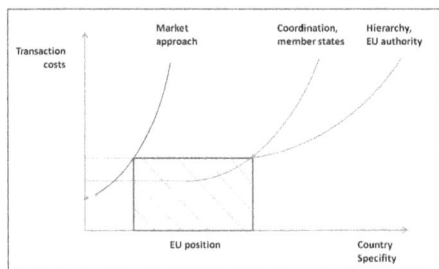

Figure 3 - Country Specifity, Transaction costs and organizational structure, comp. Williamson (2005)

3.2.2. Leviathan

Central government is as a monopolist if it has the sole decision-making power. Brennan and Buchanan (1980) shared the view that there is a natural tendency for government to expand its functions. Analogous to the market economy, **political competition** among decentralized governments can restrict this tendency and the power of a single government.

The notion of competition among local units of government was most famously treated in the Tiebout-model (Tiebout 1956). Under the assumption of at least partly mobile citizens, it introduced "exit" as another option of political competition besides "voice" (voting in elections). The effectiveness of political competition depends on the mobility of citizens and capital, and the literature is divided both over the desirability of such competition and its efficiency (Buchanan 2002; Caplan 2001; Oates 1999; Crémer, Estache, and Seabright 1996; Stiglitz 1982). In a European context, the limited mobility of Europeans does not seem to make "exit" an important factor for political competition (Pelkmans 2006, Special Eurobarometer 337). In the area of corporate taxation federal competition seems to be efficient in decreasing tax rates (Elschner and Vanborren 2009), because companies are mostly mobile. Especially as the EU is already one of the most regulated places in the world, political competition could be essential to limit the amount of regulation that is imposed.

Principal-agent models have introduced asymmetric information and imperfect monitoring to political analysis. Models are of two kinds: Either central government as principal and lower government levels as agents (Inman 2003; Levaggi 2002) , or the whole electorate as principal and governments as agents (Tommasi and Weinschelbaum 2007; Vaubel 2006; Lockwood 2005; Caplan 2001) . While the first view assumes that "local governments are largely agencies that respond to central directives" (Oates 2005, p.358), the second shows that decentralization might be welfare enhancing even with completely homogenous preferences.

The **accountability** of governments as agents to the electorate decreases with centralization (Seabright 1996), in this case when regulation is delegated to the **EU**. Different languages, geographical distance, and fewer incentives to monitor increase the leeway for public agents to maximize their own self-interest. In economic terms, it increases the costs of monitoring and at the same time decreases its benefits. For media, because voters are less interested in scandals and corruption in Brussels than in their home country. For an individual member state, because the benefits from additional monitoring are shared among all member states. *Table 1 (appx.)* provides an overview of current studies about the effects of decentralization. Most studies conclude that centralization besides slowing down economic growth increases corruption and waste. In accordance with that, the European Court of Auditors (**ECA**) until 2007 has rejected to clear the EU budget due to error and fraud for 13 consecutive years[30].

3.2.3. Lobbying

Some regard lobbying as "another case of government failure" (Ederveen, Gelauff, and Pelkmans 2008b, p.30), and related rent-seeking activities are mainly considered a negative-sum game for society (Tullock 1980). Others have argued that in a society with imperfect information, lobbyists play an important role in closing the information gap between voters and politicians (Downs 1957). Lobbying is decisive for both the desirability and the likeliness of centralization. The reason is that objectives of national lobby groups can be homogeneous or heterogeneous. For the former, centralization can increase the influence of lobby groups. For the latter, it can reduce the impact of interest groups. The influence of lobbyists does further depend on the size of an institution, on the **accountability** to the voter and the power of the bureaucracy (Vaubel 2006). Theoretical and empirical results about the influence of lobby groups are ambiguous[31] (Redoano 2010; Bordignon,

---

[30] http://news.bbc.co.uk/2/hi/europe/7092102.stm
[31] Real life examples in Europe provide support for both theories. For agricultural subsidies, the interests among most farmers are mostly homogenous, and the lobby efforts been very successful. In the case of the "Opel-Bailout", centralizing the decision-making power at Brussels can be seen as reducing lobby-influence due to conflicting interests of European carmakers.

Colombo, and Galmarini 2008; Tabellini and Wyplosz 2006; Mazza and Winden 2002; Bardhan and Mookherjee 2000).

Regarding banking regulation, on the one hand, structures and the role of municipal/state-owned banks do differ among member states. Banks that are operating in a highly regulated country might support regulation that raises the costs of rivals in other countries. Regarding hedge funds, the EU has recently passed legislation that further regulates the industry[32]. The reason could be that Hedge Funds are primarily situated in Great Britain and their lobby influence is narrowed on a European level. On the other hand, the banking industry has a strong lobby in all European countries. The push for lowering criteria to avoid negative publicity in the European bank stress test can serve as an example for the strength of the combined banking lobby on EU level[33]. All big European banks do pursue international strategies, and most have their investment banking head quarter in London. Centralizing authorities and regulation would most probably not decrease the influence of lobbyists. On the contrary, because the **accountability** is lower on **EU** level, they are, ceteris paribus, more likely to serve the purpose of the industry instead of the electorate.

3.2.4. Policy learning

In many cases, it is far from trivial to identify the optimal policy for a certain situation. "Even a government that honestly pursues the common good may not be knowledgeable or creative enough to devise the most suitable policies, or may be slow in picking up signals from society" (Ederveen, Gelauff, and Pelkmans 2008a, p.31). Decentralization leads to more diversity in policy, and enables governments to adopt the "best practices". **Yardstick competition** among local governments increases the pressure to adopt more efficient solutions (Rincke 2005). The EU open method of coordination (OMC) aims at improving this kind of policy learning (Radaelli 2003).

Regarding regulation, the exact effects of rules and standards are nearly impossible to judge in advance. Bastiat had described that every measure or law "produces not only one effect, but a series of effects"(Bastiat 1848, par 1.1). Likewise, new regulation will have direct effects, and other effects that will emerge subsequently, with unforeseen consequences. The difference between both is that "almost always (...) when the immediate consequence is favorable, the later consequences are disastrous" (Bastiat 1848, par 1.3). This is perfectly illustrated by the idea of spreading risk trough MPTS and other derivatives; the immediate consequences were growth enhancing, and the long-term effects disastrous. If regulation differs among jurisdictions, it is at least possible to test its consequences in one country before implementing it universally.

3.2.5. Complementarities

Decisions about one field of policy are often related to other fields. "Complementarities imply that a move towards centralization (...) in one dimension increases the benefit of moving in the same

---

[32] http://www.hedgefundsreview.com/hedge-funds-review/news/1725500/uk-hedge-funds-hit-eu-capital-requirements-directive
[33] http://www.spiegel.de/international/business/0,1518,708489,00.html

direction in other dimensions" (Ederveen, Gelauff, and Pelkmans 2008a, p.32). Hence, when centralizing one policy area, the marginal costs of further centralization diminish and its likelihood increases. In addition, once a central agency or bureaucracy is established, it will try to find new tasks to justify its existence (Bernholz 2009). Decisions taken may be hardly reversible. If excessive centralization is regarded as a threat (Ischia 2004), a perhaps self-enforcing dynamic must be treated with caution. With respects to upgrading three bureaucratic agencies and installing a new macro-prudential supervision organization this risk is imminent. Once a competence is centralized, experience tells that it will stay centralized. Even liberal **MEP**'s are convinced that problems with existing **EU** governance and bureaucracy can only be solved by ever more Europeanization[34].

3.2.6. Decision making

Political decision-making involves various legislative bodies, which can vary in size, terms of office and the possibility of re-election. Buchanan and Tullock (1962) have distinguished between two kinds of costs in collective decision-making. The **External-costs** function describes the costs that a minority faces, when the majority makes a decision that does negatively affect it. **Decision-making** costs are the sum of the individual efforts that are needed to achieve consent. Figure 4 simplifies real-life issues, but is nonetheless useful as an illustration. It is obvious that there is no universally applicable golden rule for decision-making, only a trade-off between imperfect alternatives.

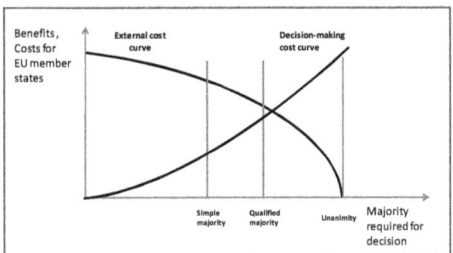

Figure 4 - Decision-making costs vs. external costs for different majority thresholds, comp. Buchanan and Tullock (1962)

For the EU, these rules play an important role. Representatives and member states feel more obliged to serving their constituency than to care for the common good (Lockwood 2005). National and local governments might be tempted to **raid the fiscal commons** (Oates 2005); cost sharing in projects might lead to an over-provision of public goods (Besley and Coate 2003), and an inefficient allocation of capital. National governments with a high standard of regulation might try to increase standards in the Union through centralization to increase their relative competiveness (Boockmann and Vaubel 2009; Vaubel 2010). If the decision-making process enables majorities to impose legislation on a minority, whose interests differ significantly, the cost can be substantial. New regulation could impose severe **external-costs** on the UK and its strong financial industry. A cost-benefit analysis should examine if this is justified by additional benefits to other member states.

---

[34] http://www.euractiv.de/finanzplatz-europa/artikel/klinz-fdp-staaten-mssen-scheinheiligkeit-aufgeben-003336

Even if more regulation were able to construct a level playing field in the EU, the adverse effect would be to weaken the EU as a whole in international competition. The pieces of the cake would be distributed more equally, but the cake would be smaller. **Political bargaining** or **logrolling** can also affect centralization. Bundling several political issues might lead to increased centralization if large minorities with a preference for centralization in a certain field of policy cooperate. One group can agree to centralization in the others' preferred field and vice versa; together the two groups can form a majority. Policies could be centralized that would not have been in single issue decisions.

3. 3. The role of the EC and the ECB

The role of the **EC** and the **ECB** is well worth its own share of the analysis. Very often, both economists and the public assume that these organizations are simply agencies that execute the function they are assigned too. Obviously, these organizations do also partly follow their own self-interest. The **EC** does not only consist of 27 commissioners, but also of thousands of bureaucrats. The same is to a smaller extent true for the **ECB**. Even if the commissioners and the **ECB**-president would always act altruistically, their bureaucracy has every (justified) interest to increase its power and secure their jobs. Empirical evidence has shown that once installed, it is hard to prevent bureaucracies from expanding their tasks and staff (Vaubel 1996b)

Assigning regulatory power to these two institutions is a safe bet on introducing new bureaucracy. If there is a weighting of regulation against a market based approach, bureaucrats are highly likely to favor new rules that fall in their competency. Again, this does not necessarily imply that they purposely choose the inferior solution. It might well be, that they assume new rules and supervision can be efficiently executed by a central agency. Over-optimism bias is a known psychological constraint, and bureaucrats are not exempt from it. The most severe objection against assigning more supervision power to central banks is its inefficiency. Neither the **FED** nor the **ECB** have foreseen the last or any of the crises before. Regarding economic forecasts, private providers deliver significantly more accurate results (Vaubel 2009). A necessary condition for more efficient forecasting is more information provision. Although the **ECB** is formally independent, there is certainly some political influence[35]. Adding financial stability to the **ECB**'s targets and giving the **EC** influence in the **ESRC** committee will definitely increase political influence on the central bank. Financial stability might conflict with its inflation target. Besides all other complaints, this measure contradicts the goal of increasing regulators independence to decrease regulatory capture.

4. The Council, Voters opinion and the risk of over-regulation

So far, it is too early to judge about regulatory reforms. It is certainly not the quantity of regulation, which caused the problem. The major risk for future stability is that politicians take the easy path and simply introduce new rules and agencies. Real problems like government interference in the housing

---

[35] Rumors had spread that the decision to purchase governments bonds[35] has been enforced mainly by the French government http://www.irishtimes.com/newspaper/breaking/2010/0510/breaking8.html

market, moral hazard problems of "Too-big-too-fail" banks, and higher and simpler capital requirements are mainly neglected or hard to implement. This chapter will deal with two issues. At first, I examine possible outcomes of the Council vote on the regulatory proposals. Under the current decision-making mechanism, most national governments are not likely to welcome new central regulation. However, specifics of **EU** decision-making bolster centralizing tendencies. Nonetheless, can we put all the blame on politics and the EU? Is it merely a problem of lacking accountability, vicious lobbies and self-serving public agents? This might not tell the whole story. Voters are, as anybody else, exposed to certain psychological constraints. New research has postulated a connection between these constraints and the risk of over-regulation.

4. 1. The Council and the political decision-making process

4.1.1. Decision making on EU level

Decision-making in supra-national Organizations or Unions is even more complex than in national states and results often differ from the original proposals. As Bismarck has famously quoted, "politics is the art of the possible". Political decisions happen in a complex environment with various stakeholder, interest groups and representatives, who each have their individual target and power. Political science has identified three kinds of power: **Decision-making power**, **agenda setting** and **preference shaping**. The most important actors in EU decision-making are the **EC**, **EP** and the **Council**. Depending on the kind of law, the process, the role of these actors and majority thresholds vary.

The **EC** possesses important agenda-setting power, as it has a monopoly on the initiative for new legislation, which "gives it considerable potential to influence the contents of legislation" (Thomson 2006, p.392). Political literature is mixed on the powers of other actors, but agrees that the **EC** has an advantage as an agenda-setter (Crombez 1997; Steunenberg, Schmidtchen, and Koboldt 1999). Nonetheless, "politically, it is not very important whether the **EP** or the **EC** is the **agenda setter**, because their positions are usually close to each other" (Tsebelis 1994, p.137). The **EP** and **EC** interests are mainly homogenous, and their combined decision-making power is higher if the member states are heterogeneous in their opinion.

Regarding the reform of banking regulation, proposals undergo a **co-decision procedure**. Thereby, **Council** and **EP** negotiate on amendments to the **EC** proposition. While power is mostly regarded as equal in this phase (Napel and Widgrén 2006), the **Council** has to make the final decision. It will have to be decided by **qualified majority**. Since the introduction of new "double majority" voting-rules [36]has been postponed until 2014, this is based on the rules established in the Nice treaty. All member states are assigned a certain number of votes[37]. A **qualified majority** requires:

-     A simple majority of member states (for proposals by **EC**)
-     A majority of 255 out of 345 votes

---

[36] http://europa.eu/scadplus/constitution/doublemajority_de.htm
[37] Appendix for exact numbers

- If requested by a member state, the approval of at least 62% of the EU population.

There is an eminent connection between the decision-making process and centralization. The **EC** has an advantage through its agenda-setting power. At the same time, it is most likely to push for further centralization. The **Council** has to react on the proposals of the commission. Of course, it can merely reject proposals. However, if it wants to pass legislation, it will have to build on the proposals of the **EC**. Figure 5 demonstrates a very simplified example, how the **Council** might accept an **EC** proposal, although its original preference was a less centralized position. More complex, game-theoretical models do not particularly add value to the current analysis (Barr and Passarelli 2009).

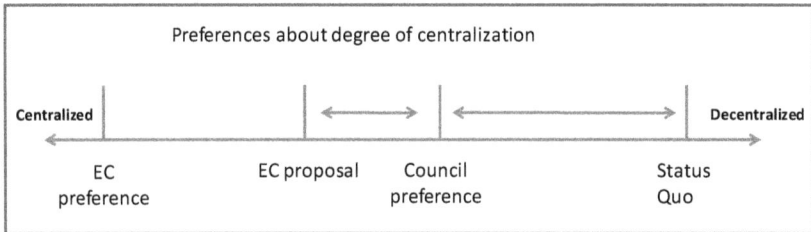

Figure 5 - Agenda-setting power of EC bolsters centralization

4.1.2. Description of data

With **EC** and the **EP** both supporting the proposals, the only institution to possibly limit centralization is the **Council**. From public statements, it is not clear which position it will take. The delay in the legislative process indicates that the member states are divided in their opinion. In an attempt to shed light on this process, I analyze the composition of the **Council** and the interest of member states. Is it likely that the proposal will pass? What are the factors that play a role in the **Council** decision? For the analysis, I rely on data from several sources. Data about voter opinion has been acquired from the Eurobarometer-Surveys, provided through the European commission. Data about regulation and economic freedom stems from the Annual Economic Freedom of the World Report 2009, available at www.freetheworld.com. Data about political orientation and the coalitions of European governments originate from the homepage of the **Council**. There is a certain sampling problem as not all data are from the exact same survey. However, the purpose of this analysis will sufficiently be achieved even with these limitations in mind.

Table 5 (appx.) provides an overview about the variables. *Table 2* shows all variables that are used to assess attributes of and facts about EU member states. Detailed descriptions can also be found there (appx. p. 39). If necessary, I refer to graphs and results. To ease its readability, I have marked the highest and lowest value on each item (UK separate). For the analysis of the Council decision important are the following variables. **FNL** and **FEL** state the preferences of voters to fight economic crises on a National or European level. Other options have been available, but are not of relevance here. **TEC** reveals trust in the European Commission. **PTM** and **PFS** reveal the preference for a more market based reform approach based on more transparency, or a government interference based approach focusing on supervision. I will use some results in the following analysis of the Council and voters in the member states. The cross-country sample consists of 27 observations, as there are 27 EU countries.

4.1.3. Application to EU Council decision-making

Modeling or predicting decisions made by and between member states is a nontrivial task. Different assessment criteria can be used to test outcomes. On a national level, political direction (left – right) can predict voting quite reliably. Nonetheless, a right-wing government in one country might be considered moderate in another. To approximate the political orientation of governments, I have used the affiliation of national parties to their European umbrella organizations. The following overview is in the order from probably opposing to supporting centralization.

- The **Alliance of European Conservatives and Reformists (AECR)** is a centre-right anti-federalist European political party
- The **European Liberal Democrat and Reform Party (LDR)** is composed of 56 national-level liberal and liberal-democratic parties
- The **European People's Party (EPP)** is a centre-right, Christian democratic political party.
- The **European Green Party (EGP)** is the Green political party at European level
- The **Party of the European Left (EL)** comprises democratic socialist and communist parties.

I created four **assessment bases (AB)** based on the likelihood of parties to support the proposal. All other parties that are not part of an **AB** are assumed to support the legislation. **AB1** is the strictest criterion, which contains only governments that clearly oppose Centralization.

- **AB1** is that an **AECR** party is part of the national government.
- **AB2** is that an **AECR** or **LDR** party is part of the national government. Liberal parties should oppose more regulation that interferes with personal and economic freedom.
- **AB3** is that the government is right wing
- **AB4** is that the government or coalition is right-wing or politically mixed.

However, it is not clear if the political orientation of governments is the best proxy for voting behavior on single issues or legislation. In regular democratic elections, voters elect a party as a bundle of political preferences. The voter is only able to select the party that he supposes is on average closest to his personal preferences in various political areas. The government on the other hand cannot really be sure what voters expect from it; and how to best ensure its re-election. An answer to this has been that "politicians can get a more nuanced reading from surveys" (Caplan 2005, p.8). Real life anecdotal evidence suggests that among others Bill Clinton relied "heavily on polls to formulate his policy views" (Genovese and Streb 2004, p.2)

It is therefore permissible to use survey results as an assessment base for the vote of a member state. This approach has been applied to decision-making in the Council before (Barr and Passarelli 2009). For the analysis, I created two dummy variables. **EON** indicates if more people in a member state prefer the **EU** level to National level (**FEL > FNL**). **SOT** indicates if people prefer

supervision to transparency (**PFS > PFM**). **AB5** is based on **EON**, and **AB6** on **SOT**.I derived my results

using the majorities needed for **Council** decisions. For each **AB** it is checked if the criteria for approval

would be met Detailed calculations in *Table 4 (appx.)*. Table 3 shows the results.

Assessment Bases AB _ Criterion	1 Political direction: No AECR party in government	2 Political direction: No AECR/ LDR party in government	3 Political direction: Government left-wing or mixed	4 Political direction: Government left wing	5 Voter opinion: European over national	6 Voter opinion: Supervision over transparency
Number of Countries in support of legislation (>=14)	23	11	12	5	18	17
Number of votes in support of legislation (>=255)	287	183	119	62	237	181
Percent of EU population (>= 62 %)	88.4%	52.7%	23.8%	14.1%	71.8%	50.2%
Criteria passed	3	0	0	0	2	1

Table 3 - Results of Council decision using different Assessment Bases

It can be seen that only under very narrow assumptions should the member states support the

proposed regulation. Only if all parties that do not contain an **AECR** party agree to it, would the

legislation pass all three criteria. If the member states base their vote on their voters' wishes, a

majority of countries would favor the legislation. However, only on the **EON AB** will the legislation

reach the population threshold. In addition, the required number of votes would in both cases not be

achieved. Under all other ABs, I would assume that governments would normally reject the proposed

changes. Nonetheless, the EC has made its proposals, and it seems unlikely that the Council will

completely reject it. Logrolling and internal consultations will play a role, it will be revealing to see

the results. Is it safe to say that the Council will block the most questionable parts of the reform?

When we look at **AB5** and **AB6**, it can be seen that this is not only a case of lacking **accountability** and

Principal-agent problems in collective decision-making. Public agents might pursue their own

interest and not necessarily the voters'. However, in a majority of member states, the voters actually

agree with the proposals and seem to prefer more Centralization and Supervision. Classical public

choice literature has mainly focused on government failures as the source of unfavorable decision.

4. 2. Voter Irrationality and the risk of over-regulation

Psychology is slowly but consistently forcing its way into economic models. Research fields like

behavioral finance or consumer behavior have now successfully adopted various psychological

concepts. One concept that could be of crucial importance in political economy is the existence of

systematic biases. Public choice has long stated that individual voters might vote unwisely due to

incomplete information (Downs 1957). Nonetheless, if voters are just rationally ignorant, and their

errors are randomly distributed, the "miracle of aggregation" leads to unbiased results (Surowiecki

2004). However, if there are **systematic biases** in individual's judgment, results do deteriorate. With concepts like rational ignorance and information economics, nearly every behavior can be explained as rational. While people seem to behave rational in most cases, there are exceptions. I use regression results from my data to highlight this problem, and show possible explanations.

If we look at *Figure* 1 in the appendix, it can be seen that the more central countries in the EU favor the **EU** level over the national level. It rather seems like people have more trust if they are merely geographically closer to an institution. Regarding the question of supervision or transparency in *Figure 2*, no clear pattern arises. A more detailed look on the numbers reveals some insight for **EON** and **SOT** (Appendix p. 11-15). Countries that prefer the European level put more trust in the **EC**, have a stronger European identity, and higher international capital controls. The predictors in a regression analysis with **EON** as dependent variable are the following: The importance of market economy/free trade has a negative effect (10% level), Economic Freedom also a negative effect (10%), Capital Controls a negative effect (5%), and trust in the **EC** a positive effect (1%). For a certain part, these results could prove differences in preferences. Voters have differing preferences for Economic Freedom and the market economy, and if their countries' status is closer to their preferences, they oppose more Europeanization. It can also be regarded as rational, that countries, which currently have a competitive advantage due to less rigorous capital controls, fear European action that might end this advantage. Such a tendency is present for countries with either very open capital markets or very strong restrictions. The other countries are "stuck-in-the-middle" and don't have clear preferences (appx. p.44). One reason why voters might favor undesirable legislation could be exemplified by the role of trust in the **EC.**

Are the preferences of voters in the **EU** compatible with a classical definition of rationality, and if not, what is the problem? This is a nontrivial question. Kahneman (2009) has proven many individual acts for which he concludes that people did not act rational. This does not prove that people are irrational. Rubin (2003) shows how people might be biased concerning economic decisions. Common sense tells people to delegate complicated tasks to institutions that they trust. Common sense also tells people that if there is a problem, there is someone to blame for, and that someone should be assigned to fix it. In our daily life life common sense is very helpful. It tells us not to trust strangers, to accept certain rules and authorities and put a big emphasis on reciprocity (Rubin 2003). In this case it could be misleading, because the **EC** might not be able to fulfil this task.

It is human to assign supervision to someone you trust instead of relying on people in markets that you do not know. This might have worked in a world "of little specialization and division of labor, little capital, low technological change, and little or no economic growth" (Rubin 2003, p.163). In such a static world regulation and supervision through central authorities makes sense. The real world economy today however is a complex system, in which actors respond to incentives and jobs are created or destroyed due to shifts in preferences and productivity. Another logical explanation for apparent individual "irrationality" could be differentiating act-rationality and rule-rationality. Nobel laureate John Aumann has argued that people do not maximize their utility for each individual act, because the cognitive costs would be too high. Instead, they rely on rules that on average maximize their utility[38]. People get along quite well with their misperceptions and biases in their daily life (Cosmides and Tooby 1992; Caplan 2001), but "in a democracy, voters who may have misconceptions about economics can vote for politicians who will implement erroneous and costly policies"(Rubin 2003, p.167). Therefore economists cannot discard psychological constraints when making policy proposals. Caplan (2001c) shows in an economic framework that people will be more likely to make sound decisions in markets, where they directly face the costs of their actions. In politics, their marginal influence is close to zero, and so are the costs of having a biased judgment.

Although people are right to put more faith in trustful persons than on strangers in their daily life, this insight leads to the wrong results deciding between regulation and a market solution.

Paul Krugman has blamed "the profession's blindness to the very possibility of catastrophic failures" (Krugman 2009, p.1). Economists "turned a blind eye to the limitations of human rationality" (Krugman 2009, p.2), because they wanted to fit everything into formal models. He correctly concludes that economists in the future will have to "acknowledge the importance of irrational and often unpredictable behavior" (Krugman 2009, p.2). Markets do not always function perfectly well, and human decisions are sometimes irrational. Nonetheless, Krugman is not wholly consistent in his analysis. He, among others, concludes that behavioral economics justifies more government intervention in markets. When people in markets are subject to "known biases in human cognition" (Krugman 2009, p.11), let the government come and fix these biases. But the same people that act in markets do run governments and work in public agencies. The problems with collective decision-making that have been outlined so far might even amplify "irrationality" on individual level.

Behavioral financial economist David Hirshleifer explains, "The behavioral approach in some ways strengthens the case for laissez-faire, and raises some new doubts about the value of regulation" (Hirshleifer 2008, p.856). He concludes that regulation is often motivated by biases, whereas the reactions of the regulated companies are mainly rational. I have made a similar argument when I stated that banks' behavior in the run up to the crisis, given the regulatory incentives, was mainly consistent with rational behavior. However existing literature has mainly ignored the fact that "regulators, politicians and voters are subject to systematic biases" (Hirshleifer 2008, p.857). Various psychological effects make voters demand more regulation than would be efficient. Does collective decision-making in the EU amplify this effect? Assuming that there are biased preferences about regulation, it is theoretically possible that they cancel one another out between different member states. However if Hirshleifer is correct and demanding too much

---

[38] Rule Rationality vs. Act Rationality ,2008 - 3rd Meeting in Economic Sciences, http://www.lindau-nobel.org/AbstractDetails.AxCMS?AbstractID=239

regulation is the norm, it is highly unlikely that biased preferences about regulation will cancel out between member states. If voters actually want more regulation, should a well functioning democratic system not provide them with more regulation? This is a difficult question. If demanding too much regulation is common, there should be checks and balances that limit harmful decisions.

A good comparison could be the field of free trade. Most voters do doubt the benefits of free trade, yet economists are in principle united in its support. The political solution to solve this problem was to engage in Free Trade Agreements and delegate the responsibility to the **WTO**. Regarding free trade, the **WTO** mainly acts as an independent judge executing the commonly agreed rules. Regarding the **EU regulatory proposal**, new central agencies would receive immense powers and would be able to develop their own agenda. While the competences of the **WTO** are clearly defined, the new **EU** institutions would have a very broad and wide range of responsibilities. Two of the institutions involved, the **EC** and the **EP,** have a clear preference for centralization that does not necessarily maximize total utility. On the contrary, de-centralization will provide at least some checks and balances. Regulatory competition will to some degree limit excessive regulation. Policy learning through different approaches will enable politicians to not apply all rules at once, but rather wait for their success in other countries. It could be easier to indentify responsibilities for regulatory failure.

5. Conclusion

The debate about reforming banking regulation in the EU focuses on more rules and additional bureaucracies. It advocates encouraging "currently poorly regulated or "uncooperative" jurisdictions to adhere to the highest level international standard" (The De Larosière Group 2009, p.66). Following this logic, it was the low level of regulation, which did cause the crisis. However, banking is the most heavily regulated industry sector since the Great depression, which did not to help prevent any of the many banking crises. The quintessence is that, the more complicated the rules, the higher the incentives to circumvent them and the more inefficient they are.

Empirically, compliance with Basel principles has not yet been shown to increase bank soundness and reduce systemic risk (Demirguc-Kunt and Detragiache 2010). Heizo Takenaka, a former Japanese minister for regulation, said "it would be foolish to expect smart regulation (...) in the current populist climate (...) it is impossible for politicians to understand finance" [39] All reform proposals that rely on more supervision and more rules have a problem: Rules can be circumvented and will be if the incentives are wrong. While Goldman Sachs has already developed their strategy to circumvent new rules and stated, "The impact will be minimal"[40], both politicians and voters favor more and centralized regulation. The reason lies partly in psychological constraints and biases, partly in the desire of political institutions to increase their power. Centralization is likely to amplify this bias for over-regulation, because there is more leeway for regulatory capture, lobby groups and

---

[39] http://www.acus.org/new_atlanticist/davos-2010-no-agreement-bank-regulation
[40] http://www.businessweek.com/news/2010-07-29/goldman-confident-reform-law-is-manageable-bofa-says.html

25

bureaucratic inefficiency. Decentralization on the other hand provides a constraining element in the form of political competition. Moreover, it is easier for the media and voters to detect corruption and the influence of lobby groups on regulators and supervisors.

This is not to say that no reform is necessary. On the contrary, but centralization that causes more bureaucracy and less **accountability** is the wrong way. National agencies are very well able to execute regulatory reforms. The German authorities have single-handedly banned some kinds of uncovered short sales. Increasing budgets and offering better salaries to attract regulators that are more capable is also possible on a national level. George Soros has emphasized "separating commercial and investment banking" instead of "hasty and ill-considered regulations".[41]A first draft of new U.S. regulation included the so-called Volcker-Rule. It would have stopped big banks from engaging in proprietary trading, however it does not seem to "be nowhere at all in the list of priorities"[42] for the U.S. Treasury. The emphasis of an effective reform must be on simple rules and enforcing transparency. Re-instating the risk of bankruptcy would change the parameters in the banks' and rating agencies' risk models. Risk would become less attractive. Hellwig (2010) has argued for simpler, stricter and higher capital requirements. In addition, banks must be forced to disclose more information publicly instead of secretly hiding it in the back offices of regulatory agencies.

Krugman (2009) was correct in asserting that markets are not perfectly and strongly efficient. At the same time, an overwhelming amount of studies has proven that markets are very efficient and quick in processing past and public information (Surowiecki 2004). Decreasing the costs of information procurement by publicly disclosing it will improve the anticipation of bubbles and mispricing. No single agency, might it be as well equipped as possible, can provide the same amount of intellectual capacity as the sum of all actors in a market. According to Hayek, the necessary "knowledge of the circumstances ( ) never exists in concentrated or integrated form (Hayek 1945, p.519), thus such a problem "cannot possibly be solved by any particular person or board" (Sunstein 2007, p.89). While other fields like computer science, biology and even physics do now embrace the concept of collective intelligence, the new EU regulation should not be based on concepts of the last century. A reform should oblige banks to publish more information. It should mainly stop commercials banks from engaging in trading. New capital requirements must be simple and provide no incentives for regulatory arbitrage. Parts of such reforms can be seen as a burden and as a competitive disadvantage for national banks. Every country does continue to negotiate for the most convenient rules for "its" banks[43]. However, after billion-dollar bailouts, taxpayers are obliged to ask for reforms that will limit their risk exposure and assign responsibility back to the shareholders of banks. New regulation and rules as outlined above could have a real positive effect; they would not just serve as a placebo for the public.

[4141] http://news.bbc.co.uk/2/hi/business/8483328.stm
[42] http://baselinescenario.com/2010/08/05/the-treasury-position-on-the-volcker-rule/
[43] http://www.spiegel.de/wirtschaft/unternehmen/0,1518,713847,00.html

26

V. Bibliography

Citation style (American Political Science Review)

Akai, N. 2002. "Fiscal decentralization contributes to economic growth: evidence from state-level cross-section data for the United States." *Journal of Urban Economics* 52(1): 93-108.

Akerlof, GA, and RJ Shiller. 2010. "Animal spirits: how human psychology drives the economy, and why it matters for global capitalism."

Artés, Joaquín, and Enrique García Viñuela. 2007. "Campaign spending and office-seeking motivations: an empirical analysis." *Public Choice* 133(1-2): 41-55.

Avgouleas, Emilios. 2009. "Financial Innovation Versus Systemic Stability." *About Lombard Street* 1(11).

Baltensperger, Ernst. 2003. "Competition of Bank Regulators : A More Optimistic View . A Comment on the Paper by Hans-Werner Sinn." *Finanzarchiv*: 330-335.

Bardhan, P., and D. Mookherjee. 2000. "Capture and governance at local and national levels." *American Economic Review* 151(3712): 135–139.

Barr, Jason, and Francesco Passarelli. 2009. "Who has the power in the EU ?." *Mathematical Social Sciences* 57: 339-366.

Barth, JR, G Caprio, and R Levine. 2006. "Rethinking bank regulation: till angels govern." *Journal of International Development* 19(8): 1166-1168.

Bastiat, Frederic. 1848. *Selected Essays on Political Economy*. Irvington-on-Hudson. , NY: The Foundation for Economic Education, Inc.

Bernholz, P, and R Vaubel. 2004. "Political competition, innovation and growth in the history of Asian civilizations."

Bernholz, Peter. 2009. "Are international organizations like the Bank for International Settlements unable to die?." *The Review of International Organizations* 4(4): 361-381.

Besley, T, and S. Coate. 2003. "Centralized versus decentralized provision of local public goods: a political economy approach." *Journal of public economics* 87(12): 2611–2637.

Boehm, Frédéric. 2007. "Regulatory Capture Revisited–Lessons from Economics of Corruption." *North*.

Boockmann, Bernhard, and Roland Vaubel. 2009. "The Theory of Raising Rivals' Costs and Evidence from the International Labour Organisation." *World Economy* 32(6): 862-887.

Bordignon, M, L Colombo, and U Galmarini. 2008. "Fiscal federalism and lobbying." *Journal of Public Economics* 92(12): 2288-2301.

Brennan, G, and JM Buchanan. 1980. "The power to tax: Analytical foundations of a fiscal constitution."

Brennan, G., and J. Buchanan. 1984. "Voter Choice: Evaluating Political Alternatives." *American Behavioral Scientist* 28(2): 185-201.

Brumbaugh Jr, R.D., and R.E. Litan. 1989. "The S & L Crisis: How to Get out and Stay Out." *The Brookings Review* 7(2): 3–13.

Buchanan, J.M. 2002. "Fiscal equalization revisited." *Atlantic Institute for Market Studies* (April).

Buchanan, JM, and G Tullock. 1962. "The calculus of consent: Logical foundations of constitutional democracy."

Bó, E Dal. 2006. "Regulatory capture: a review." *Oxford Review of Economic Policy* 22(2): 203-225.

Calem, PS, and M Lacour-Little. 2004. "Risk-based capital requirements for mortgage loans." *Journal of Banking & Finance* 28(3): 647-672.

Caplan, B. 2005. "From Friedman to Wittman: The transformation of Chicago political economy." *Scholarly Comments on Academic Economics* 2(1): 1–21.

Caplan, B. 2001. "Has Leviathan been bound? A theory of imperfectly constrained government with evidence from the states." *Southern Economic Journal* 11(1): 67.

Caplan, Bryan. 2001. "Rational irrationality and the microfoundations of political failure." *Public Choice* 107(3-4): 311-331.

Caplan, Bryan. 2001. "Standing Tiebout on his head: tax capitalization and the monopoly power of local governments." *Public Choice* 108(1-2): 101-122.

Corgel, John B., and Gerald D. Gay. 1987. "Local Economic Base, Geographic Diversification, and Risk Management of Mortgage Portfolios." *Real Estate Economics* 15(3): 256-267.

Cosmides, Leda, and John Tooby. 1992. "Cognitive Adaptations for Social Exchange." *Social Science.*

Crombez, C. 1997. "The co-decision procedure in the European Union." *Legislative Studies Quarterly* 22(1): 97–119.

Crémer, J, A Estache, and P Seabright. 1996. "Decentralizing public services: What can we learn from the theory of the firm." *Revue d'economie politique.*

Demirguc-Kunt, A, and Enrica Detragiache. 2010. "Basel core principles and bank soundness: does compliance matter?." *Journal of Financial Stability.*

Downs, Anthony. 1957. "An Economic Theory of Political Action in a Democracy." *Journal of Political Economy* 65(2): 135.

Dreher, Axel, and Roland Vaubel. 2004. "Do IMF and IBRD cause moral hazard and political business cycles? Evidence from panel data." *Open Economies Review.*

Ederveen, Sjef, George Gelauff, and Jacques Pelkmans. 2008." Assessing Subsidiarity." In *Subsidiarity and Economic Reform in Europe*, , p. 19-40.

Eller, Markus. 2004. "The determinants of fiscal decentralisation and its impact on economic growth: Empirical evidence from a panel of OECD countries." *Unpublished Master Thesis, University of Vienna* (0).

Elschner, C, and W Vanborren. 2009. *Corporate Effective Tax Rates in an Enlarged European Union.*

Enikolopov, Ruben, and Ekaterina Zhuravskaya. 2007. "Decentralization and political institutions." *Journal of Public Economics* 91(11-12): 2261-2290.

Fabozzi, F.J. 2001. *The handbook of mortgage-backed securities.* McGraw-Hill Companies.

Fisman, R. 2002. "Decentralization and corruption: evidence across countries." *Journal of Public Economics* 83(3): 325-345.

Fresh, Adriane;, and Martin N. Baily. 2009. "FinReg21." *What does international experience tells us about regulatory consolidation.* Available at: http://www.finreg21.com/lombard-street/what-does-international-experience-tell-us-about-regulatory-consolidation.

Frey, BS. 2009. "The public choice view of international political economy." *International Organization* 38(01): 199 -223.

Gadinis, Stavros. 2008. "The Politics of Competition in International Financial Regulation." *Harvard International Law Journal* 49(2).

Genovese, Michael A., and Matthew Justin Streb. 2004. *Polls and politics: the dilemmas of democracy.* SUNY Press.

Gintis, Herbert. 2009. "Animal Spirits or Complex Adaptive Dynamics? A Review of George Akerlof and Robert J. Schiller Animal Spirits (Princeton, 2009)." *Central European*: 1-11.

Group30. 2009. "Financial Reform: A Framework for Financial Stability - Group of Thirty."

Hayek, FA Von. 1945. "The use of knowledge in society." *American Economic Review*: 1-11.

Hellwig, Martin F. 2009. "Systemic Risk in the Financial Sector: An Analysis of the Subprime-Mortgage Financial Crisis." *De Economist* 157(2): 129-207.

Hellwig, Martin. 2010. "Capital Regulation after the Crisis : Business as Usual ?."

Hirshleifer, David. 2008. "Psychological Bias as a Driver of Financial Regulation." *European Financial Management* 14(5): 856-874.

Inman, RP. 2003." Transfers and bailouts: Enforcing local fiscal discipline with lessons from US federalism." In *Fiscal decentralization and the challenge of hard budget constraints*, Jennie Ilene Litvack Jonathan Rodden, Gunnar S. Eskeland. MIT.

Ischia, H. 2004. *Zentralisierung und Subsidiarität.* Lang, Peter Frankfurt.

Kahneman, D. 2009. "New challenges to the rationality assumption." *Legal Theory.*

Krugman, P. 2009. "How did economists get it so wrong?." *The New York Times* 6: 2009.

Levaggi, R. 2002. "Decentralized Budgeting Procedures for Public Expenditure." *Public Finance Review.*

Lockwood, Ben. 2005. *Fiscal decentralization: A political economy perspective.*

Macher, JT, and BD Richman. 2008. "Transaction cost economics: An assessment of empirical research in the social sciences." *Business and Politics* 10(1).

Mazza, Isidoro, and F.V. Winden. 2002. "Does centralization increase the size of government? The effects of separation of powers and lobbying." *International Tax and Public Finance* 9(4): 379–389.

Mueller, G.R., and B.A. Ziering. 1992. "Real estate portfolio diversification using economic diversification." *Journal of Real Estate Research* 7(4): 375–386.

Napel, Stefan, and Mika Widgrén. 2006. "The Inter-Institutional Distribution of Power in EU Codecision." *Social Choice and Welfare* 27(1): 129-154.

Niskanen, WA. 1971. "Bureaucracy and Representative Government. 1971."

Oates, W.E. 2005. "Toward a second-generation theory of fiscal federalism." *International Tax and Public Finance* 12(4): 349–373.

Oates, Wallace E. 1999. "An essay on fiscal federalism." *Journal of economic literature* 37(3): 1120-1149.

Oates, Wallace. 1972. "Fiscal federalism." *New York.*

Ogden, William, Nanda Rangan, and Thomas Stanley. 1989. "Risk reduction in S&L mortgage loan portfolios through geographic diversification." *Journal of Financial Services Research* 2(1): 39-48.

Pelkmans, Jacques. 2006." Testing For Subsidiarity." In *Die Europäische Union: Innere Verfasstheit und globale Handlungsfähigkeit*, BEEP briefing, Thomas Bruha and Carsten Nowak. Nomos Baden-Baden.

Peltzman, Sam. 2010. "Regulation and the Natural Progress of Opulence." *Economic Affairs* (September).

Radaelli, CM. 2003. "The open method of co-ordination: a new governance architecture for the European Union?: preliminary report." *Svenska institutet for europapolitiska.*

Redoano, Michela. 2010. "Does centralization affect the number and size of lobbies?." *Journal of Public Economic Theory* 12(3): 407–435.

Rincke, Johannes. 2005. *Yardstick competition and policy innovation.*

Rodden, Jonathan. 2003. "Reviving Leviathan: Fiscal Federalism and the Growth of Government." *International Organization* 57(04): 695-729.

Rubin, PH. 2003. "Folk Economics.." *Southern Economic Journal* 70(1): 157-171.

Seabright, Paul. 1996. "Accountability and decentralisation in government : An incomplete contracts model." *European Economic Review* 40: 61-89.

Sinn, Hans-Werner. 2003. "Risktaking, Limited Liability, and the Competition of Bank Regulators." *FinanzArchiv* 59(3): 305-329.

Sinn, Hans-werner. 2003. "Asymmetric Information, Bank Failures, ant the Rationale for Harmonizing Banking Regulation. A rejoinder on Comments of Ernst Baltensperger and Peter Spencer." *Finanzarchiv*: 340-346.

Stansel, D. 2005. "Local decentralization and local economic growth: A cross-sectional examination of US metropolitan areas." *Journal of Urban Economics* 57(1): 55-72.

Steunenberg, B., D. Schmidtchen, and C. Koboldt. 1999. "Strategic power in the European Union: evaluating the distribution of power in policy games." *Journal of Theoretical Politics* 11: 339–366.

Stigler, GJ. 1971. "The theory of economic regulation." *The Bell journal of economics and management* 2(1): 3-21.

Stiglitz, JE. 1982. "The theory of local public goods twenty-five years after Tiebout: A perspective." *NBER working paper*.

Sunstein, Cass R. 2007. "Neither Hayek nor Habermas." *Public Choice* 134(1-2): 87-95.

Surowiecki, J. 2004. "The wisdom of crowds: Why the many are smarter than the few and how collective wisdom shapes business, economies." *Societies and Nations*.

Tabellini, Guido, and Charles Wyplosz. 2006. "Supply-side policy coordination in the European Union." *Swedish Economic Policy Review* 13(1): 101.

The De Larosière Group. 2009. "The high-level group on financial supervison in the EU."

Thiessen, U. 2003. "Fiscal decentralisation and economic growth in high-income OECD countries." *Fiscal Studies* 52(3): 507-522.

Thomson, R. 2006. "Who Has Power in the EU? The Commission, Council and Parliament in Legislative Decision-making*." *Journal of common market studies* 44(2): 391.

Thornton, J. 2007. "Fiscal decentralization and economic growth reconsidered☆." *Journal of Urban Economics* 61(1): 64-70.

Tiebout, CM. 1956. "A pure theory of local expenditures." *The journal of political economy* 64(5): 416-424.

Tocqueville, A De. 1863. "Democracy In America--Vol. 1."

Tommasi, Mariano, and Federico Weinschelbaum. "Centralization vs . Decentralization : A Principal-Agent Analysis." *Analysis*: 1-28.

Tommasi, Mariano, and Federico Weinschelbaum. 2007. "Centralization vs. Decentralization: A Principal-Agent Analysis." *Journal of Public Economic Theory* 9(2): 369-389.

Treisman, Daniel. 2002. "Decentralization and the Quality of Government." *unpublished paper, Department of Political Science, UCLA* (October 2002).

Tsebelis, George. 1994. "The Power of the European Parliament as a Conditional Agenda Setter." *The American Political Science Review* 88(1): 128 - 142.

Tullock, G. 1980. "Rent seeking as a negative-sum game." *Toward a Theory of the Rent–Seeking Society*.

Tullock, G. 1967. "The welfare costs of monopolies, tariffs and theft." *Western Economic Journal*.

Tullock, Gordon. 1998. "Externalities and government." *Public Choice*: 3-4.

Vaubel, Roland. 1996. "Bureaucracy at the IMF and the World Bank: A Comparison of the Evidence." *World Economy*.

Vaubel, Roland. 2008. "Constitutional Courts as Promoters of Political Centralization : Lessons for the European Court of Justice." (0049): 1-29.

Vaubel, Roland. 1996. "Constitutional Safeguards Against Centralization in Federal States : An International Cross-Section Analysis." *New York* 102: 79-102.

Vaubel, Roland. 2010. "Die Finanzkrise als Vorwand für Überregulierung." *Wirtschaftsdienst* 90(5): 313-320.

Vaubel, Roland. 2009. "Lessons From the Financial Crisis: the International Dimension." *Economic Affairs* 29(3): 22-26.

Vaubel, Roland. 2006. "Principal-agent problems in international organizations." *The Review of International Organizations* (September 2005): 125-138.

Vaubel, Roland. 1994. "The political economy of centralization and the European Community." *Public Choice* 81(1): 151–190.

Vaubel, Roland. 2008. "The political economy of labor market regulation by the European Union." *The Review of International Organizations*.

Wallison, P.J., and B. Ely. 2000. *Nationalizing Mortgage Risk: The Growth of Fannie Mae and Freddie Mac*. American Enterprise Institute.

Williamson, Oliver E. 2005. "The Economics of Governance." *American Economic Review* 95(2): 1-18.

Yandle, B. 1983. "Bootleggers and Baptists: The education of a regulatory economist." *Regulation* 7(3): 12–16.

Ölschläger, Jessica. 2010. "Wie wirken sich Steuersysteme auf die Wettbewerbsfähigkeit von Volkswirtschaften aus?." *Wirtschaftsdienst* 90(6): 415-419.

VI. Appendix

Tables

Figures

Table 4: Current studies on the effects of decentralization

34

Paper	Method	Data	Dependent variable	Independent variables (+ control variables)	Results
(Akai 2002)	Panel data analysis	50 states in the US, 1992-1996	- Economic growth, - State level	- Revenue indicator - Production indicator - Autonomy indicator - Production-revenue indicator	Fiscal decentralization contributes to economic growth
(Stansel 2005)	Cross-section OLS regression	314 US metropolitan areas, 1960 -1990	- Economic growth, - Population growth	- Central-city share of metro area population - number of municipalities per 100,000 residents - number of counties per 100,000 residents	All independent variables associated with decentralization are significantly positively related to economic growth
(Thornton 2007)	Panel data analysis, Logarithmic OLS	19 OECD countries, 1980-2000	- Economic growth	- average tax revenues of sub-national governments stemming over which they have full discretion	If the measure of fiscal decentralization is limited to the revenues over which sub-national governments have full autonomy, its impact on economic growth is not statistically significant
(Eller 2004)	Panel data, country and time-fixed effects	22 OECD Countries, 1972 -1996	- Economic growth	- the sub-national governments' share in general government expenditures net of intergovernmental transfers, - sub-national government's share in total government revenues	High-income and high middle-income OECD countries show a positive growth performance when they converge to a medium degree of expenditure decentralization
(Enikolopov and Zhuravskaya 2007)	Panel data, country-fixed effects regressions	53 – 70 OECD Countries, 1975 – 2000	- Index of corruption as proxy for quality of government - Economic growth - Quality of public goods provision	- Strength of national political parties - Dummy variables indicating whether municipal and provincial executives are elected or appointed - Share of subnational revenues in total government revenues	- Strength of national political parties significantly improves outcomes of fiscal decentralization - Administrative subordination does not improve the results of fiscal decentralization

Table 4: Current studies on the effects of decentralization

Study	Method	Sample	Dependent variables	Independent variables	Results
(Rodden 2003)	Panel data, Log-regression with fixed country effects	22 Countries, 1978-1997	- Total public-sector expenditure as a percent of GDP	- Central revenue - Grants - Subnational own-sources	- Decentralization, when funded primarily by autonomous local taxation is associated with a smaller public sector
(Boockmann and Vaubel 2009)	Panel data,	123 ILO voting comitees, 1980-1997	- proportion of votes a government has cast in favor of tightening a proposed ILO convention	- Government voting in line with voters and/ or employers - Level of domestic regulation - Left-wing government - exporter of low-skilled labor intensive goods	- Governments vote for tighter standards in ILO if labor regulation is high in their own country, - Left-wing governments vote more in line with unions
(Olschläger 2010)	Panel data analysis	30 OECD Countries, 1990-2005	- current account balance, - foreign direct investments, - Economic growth	- Share of direct taxes/GDP - Share of indirect taxes/GDP	- Taxes are a part of locational competition - Direct taxes are negatively related to economic growth, negatively related to direct investments, and positively related to current account balance
(Eischner and Vanborren 2009)	Panel data analysis	27 EU member countries, 1998-2007	- Effective tax burden	- Statutory corporation tax rates - Corporate real estate taxes, net wealth taxes and other non-profit taxes on assets - Capital allowances for industrial buildings, machinery, intangibles and the tax treatment of financial assets and inventories.	- Effective tax rate is sig. higher in old than in new member states - There is no convergence of rates - Considerable downward trend in tax rates - Corporate tax competition seems to be higher in the EU than in Japan, the US and Canada
(Thiessen 2003)	Cross-section OLS regression, average annual data	High-income OECD Countries, 1973-1998	- Economic growth - Total investment share in GDP - Total factor productivity growth	- subnational share of total government spending - Subnational share of total government revenues	- There is an optimal level of fiscal decentralization - Countries converge towards an intermediate level of decentralization - The effect of decentralization on growth is inversed U-shaped

Table 4: Current studies on the effects of decentralization

(Fisman 2002)	Cross section OLS regression	59 Countries, 1980-1995	- International Country Risk Guide's corruption index	- Subnational share of total government spending - Subnational share of total government revenues	- Strong and consistent negative association between decentralization and corruption
(Treisman 2002)	OLS regression, WLS regression,		- Transparency International's corruption perceptions index - World Bank corruption Index - Quality of government quality (not efficiency)44	- Dummy: at least one policy area exclusively to subnational governments - Subnational share of total government spending - Dummy: Subnational executive elected or appointed - Dummy: Regionally chosen upper house of parliament - Number of tiers of government	- Several types of decentralization tend to reduce the quality of government, and perceived corruption - States with a larger number of tiers tend to have higher perceived corruption

---

[44] Not including cost efficiency makes the results significantly less meaningful. The claim of Tiebout competition and other arguments is especially that decentralization increases efficiency, not the level of public good provision

Table 5: Overview of variables for the 27 EU Countries – Highest and lowest highlighted

Countries	Fight crisis on National level	Fight Crisis on EU level	Trust in European Commission	Existence of European Identity	Priority: Transparency on financial markets	Priority: Stronger Financial supervision
	FNL	FEL	TEC	EEI	PTM	PFS
Austria	21	19	46	78	22	21
Belgium	11	24	58	83	21	36
Bulgaria	32	26	59	**59**	32	36
Czech Republic	20	16	59	78	16	36
Denmark	**6**	19	55	86	29	27
Estonia	12	25	62	85	34	26
Finland	15	20	57	85	26	36
France	15	26	50	72	29	21
Germany	25	24	43	87	25	32
Greece	16	21	51	79	18	23
Hungary	29	21	54	87	17	**16**
Ireland	13	15	39	74	37	23
Italy	19	25	51	68	29	21
Latvia	17	26	49	77	31	33
Lithuania	14	19	**38**	62	27	44
Luxembourg	14	34	59	89	22	23
Malta	20	22	55	76	31	34
Netherlands	39	**14**	61	78	22	**45**
Poland	16	34	48	76	21	17
Portugal	13	30	61	80	25	17
Republic of Cyprus	17	32	56	64	18	38
Romania	38	26	58	81	20	30
Slovakia	11	30	**64**	**90**	18	41
Slovenia	12	20	46	80	**11**	41
Spain	**23**	**44**	58	78	**39**	**45**
Sweden	25	15	49	88	18	44
United Kingdom	21	**10**	**21**	**48**	**19**	**21**
European Union 27	22	22	46	74	26	26

Table 5: Overview of variables for the 27 EU Countries – Highest and lowest highlighted

Countries	EU protects me against Globalization	Importance of free trade/market economy	State intervenes too much in my life	International Capital Market Controls	Regulation of Credit, Labor, and Business	Economic Freedom Index
	EPG	IME	SML	ICC	RCB	EFI
Austria	44	32	53	5.5	6.9	7.7
Belgium	53	32	67	6.4	6.9	7.2
Bulgaria	55	46	43	6.6	7.3	**6.7**
Czech Republic	47	36	60	5.4	6.8	7.1
Denmark	61	35	58	7.9	**8.2**	7.7
Estonia	55	36	44	7.5	7.4	7.8
Finland	55	30	**38**	5.7	7.0	7.6
France	50	22	58	6.7	7.0	7.4
Germany	47	37	57	5.7	**6.1**	7.5
Greece	42	32	58	5.1	**6.1**	7.1
Hungary	55	27	**75**	5.9	7.0	7.3
Ireland	**28**	21	63	**8.8**	7.4	**8.0**
Italy	50	30	65	6.5	6.3	7.0
Latvia	45	53	49	7.2	7.5	7.2
Lithuania	32	**55**	66	6.2	6.8	7.4
Luxembourg	52	20	46	6.7	7.5	7.7
Malta	47	38	54	8.0	6.9	7.5
Netherlands	44	33	63	8.6	7.3	7.6
Poland	50	32	51	4.3	6.4	6.8
Portugal	48	13	71	6.7	6.3	7.2
Republic of Cyprus	55	26	51	6.8	5.8	7.4
Romania	59	41	53	7.4	6.7	6.8
Slovakia	**62**	35	62	7.1	7.0	7.5
Slovenia	43	32	74	6.2	6.8	6.9
Spain	46	**19**	71	**5.0**	6.7	7.3
Sweden	49	29	60	5.9	7.0	7.3
United Kingdom	**39**	**32**	**74**	**8.3**	**7.8**	**7.9**
European Union 27	46	31	61	-	-	-

Variable description

FNL and **FEL** state the preferences of voters to fight economic crises on a National or European level. Other options have been available, but are not of relevance here. **TEC** reveals trust in the European Commission, and **EEI** the existence of a "European Identity" in the member states. Both are a good proxy for the attitude of citizens towards Europe. **PTM** and **PFS** reveal the preference for a more market based reform approach based on more transparency, or a government interference based approach focusing on supervision. **EPG, IME** and **SML** are items that measure the attitude of citizens towards competition and the role of the state. **EPG** is the perceived protection from globalization through the EU; **IME** the general importance of Free Trade and the market economy; and **SML** the perception of excessive state intervention in individuals lives. **ICC, RCB** and **EFI** are indices of economic freedom. **ICC** captures international capital market controls and **RCB** the overall regulation of Credit, labor and business. **EFI** is the aggregated economic freedom index. For **ICC, RCB,** and **EFI** the higher the index values, the more open, unregulated, and free the economy is.

I will use some results in the following analysis of the Council and voters in the member states. The cross-country sample consists of 27 observations, as there are 27 EU countries.

Overview of votes in EU Council

Countries	Votes
Malta	3
Luxemburg, Cyprus, Estonia, Slovenia, Latvia	4
Lithuania, Ireland, Finland, Denmark, Slovakia	7
Austria, Sweden, Bulgaria	10
Portugal, Hungary, Belgium, Czech Republic, Greece	12
Netherlands	13
Romania	14
Poland, Spain	27
Italy, France, Great Britain, Germany	29
Absolute number of votes	345

Table 6 – Voting rights in EU Council

European People's Party (EPP), a centre-right, Christian democratic European political party.

European Liberal Democrat and Reform Party is composed of 56 national-level liberal and liberal-democratic parties from across Europe

Alliance of European Conservatives and Reformists (AECR) is a centre-right anti-federalist European political party

The **European Green Party (or European Greens or EGP)** is the Green political party at European level

The **Party of the European Left**, commonly abbreviated to just the European Left, is a political party at European level and an association of democratic socialist and communist political parties in the European Union

Table 7: Calculation of Council decisions due to the three majority criteria

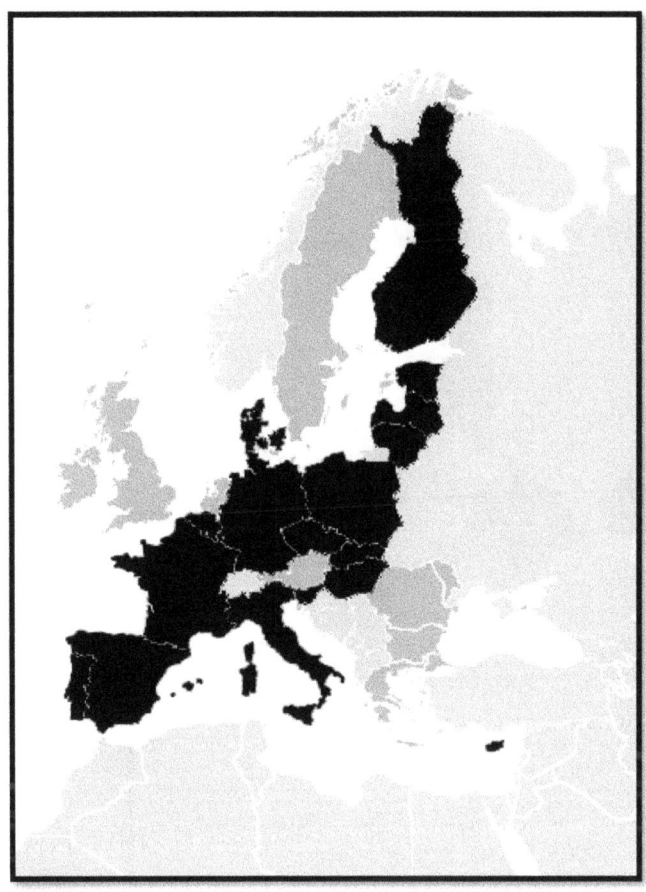

■   Prefer European level to fight crises

▨   Prefer National level to fight crises

▢   No EU member state

Source: Standard Eurobarometer 72

Question: In your opinion, which of the following is best able to take effective actions against the effects of the financial and economic crisis?

-   The European Union
-   The (National) Government

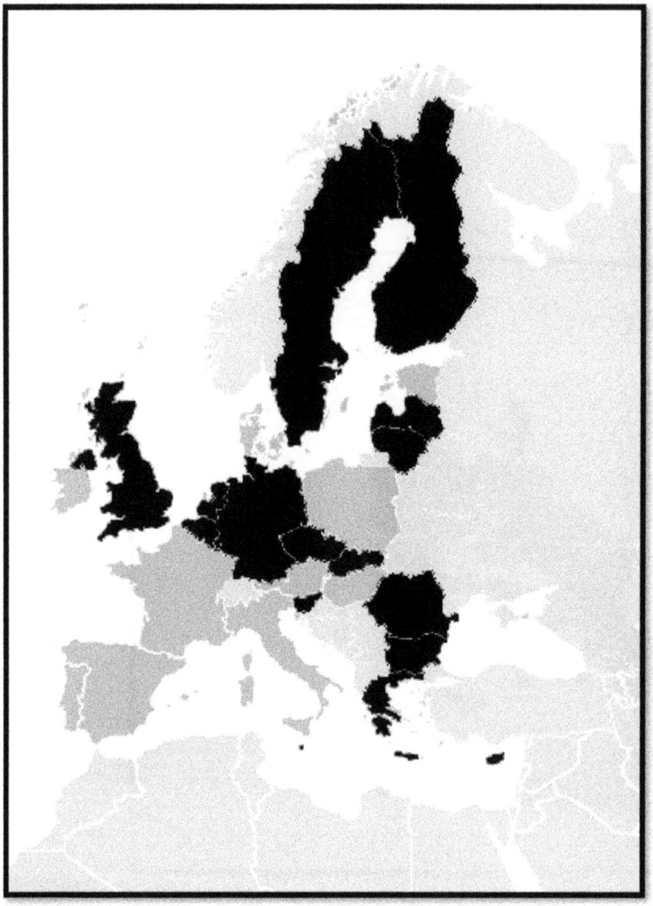

 Prefer Reform that increases supervision

 Prefer National that increases transparency

No EU member state

Source: Standard Eurobarometer 72

From the following list of measures, which one should be given priority when it comes to reforming the financial system in the European Union?

- Stronger European system of supervision of financial markets and financial institutions
- Transparency of benefits, costs and risks on financial markets

Further analysis of the data in *Table 2*

To ease the readability of *Table 2*, I have marked the highest and lowest value on each item. Due to the special standing of the UK, it is highlighted separately. The marked fields are therefore highest or lowest when disregarding the UK. Data about voter opinion has been acquired from the Eurobarometer-Surveys, provided through the European commission. Data about regulation and economic freedom stems from the Annual Economic Freedom of the World Report 2009, available at www.freetheworld.com. Data about the political orientation and the coalitions of European governments originate from the Homepage of the European Council. There is a certain sampling problem as not all data are from the exact same survey. Items 1-7 were collected 10-11.2009, Items 8-9 6-9.2009. The latest data available about economic freedom are from 2007.

For the purpose of projecting the Council decision, two binary variables EON (Europe over National) and SOT (Supervision over Transparency) were created. EON was created through using the variables FEL and FNL, SOT using PTM and PFS. Besides the calculation of the majorities that can be seen in Table 4, additional insight can be gained from the data. The following parts cover the differences in preferences between member states and relationships between the variables.

Relationship between voters' opinions and economic circumstances

```
Summary statistics: mean
   by categories of: EON (Eu over National)

  EON |      TEC       SML       IME       EEI       ICC       RCB       EFI
------+-------------------------------------------------------------------------
    0 |  48.77778  57.88889  33.77778  73.44444  71.43334  70.64444  73.95556
    1 |  53.77778  59.05556  31.66667  79.27778  63.36111  68.53333  73.31667
------+-------------------------------------------------------------------------
Total |  52.11111  58.66667  32.37037  77.33333  66.05185  69.23704  73.52963
```

This analysis relies on the binary variable EON. It is 1 if voters in a member state favor European action to the National level. It can be seen that countries, which favor the European level, differ in some variables from the others:

-   Trust in the European commission is significantly higher

-   The perception that the state interferes too much in individuals lives is slightly higher

-   The importance of a market economy/free trade is slightly lower

-   The feeling of being European/ existence of a European identity is more wide spread.

-   The International capital controls are higher

-   Regulation of credit, labor and business is slightly lower

-   The composite Economic Freedom Index does not differ

Similar relations are found when using the continuous variable FEL and its correlation to the same variables. I did run some regressions to detect possible explanations for the differing preferences about the desirability of European action. Due to severe autocorrelations, I can only test few variables at a time. The sample size is very limited, which might affect the reliability of the results. The interpretations are therefore at least partly subjective and do not claim to be definite answers.

```
reg FEL  SML IME

    Source |       SS        df        MS              Number of obs =      27
-----------+----------------------------------         F(  2,   24) =     1.95
     Model |  195.671597       2   97.8357987          Prob > F      =   0.1643
  Residual |  1204.84692      24   50.201955           R-squared     =   0.1397
-----------+----------------------------------         Adj R-squared =   0.0680
     Total |  1400.51852      26   53.8660969          Root MSE      =   7.0853


       FEL |      Coef.   Std. Err.      t    P>|t|     [95% Conf. Interval]
-----------+----------------------------------------------------------------
       SML |  -.1982281   .1443481    -1.37   0.182    -.496148    .0996917
       IME |  -.2658855   .1527141    -1.74   0.094    -.581072    .0493009
     _cons |   43.82879   11.00049     3.98   0.001    21.12489    66.53269
```

At first, it can be seen that the importance of free trade/market economy is negatively correlated to FEL, significant at the 10% level. Centralizing power might create more bureaucracy and negatively affect the market economy. On the other hand, citizens do not seem to automatically relate the EU with more interference in their personal life. Another interpretation could be that citizens who value their individual freedom oppose state intervention regardless of its level.

```
reg FEL  EEI EFI

    Source |       SS        df        MS              Number of obs =      27
-----------+----------------------------------         F(  2,   24) =     2.02
     Model |  202.178601       2   101.0893            Prob > F      =   0.1540
  Residual |  1198.33992      24   49.9308299          R-squared     =   0.1444
-----------+----------------------------------         Adj R-squared =   0.0731
     Total |  1400.51852      26   53.8660969          Root MSE      =   7.0662


       FEL |      Coef.   Std. Err.      t    P>|t|     [95% Conf. Interval]
-----------+----------------------------------------------------------------
       EEI |   .1534968   .1391445     1.10   0.281    -.1336832    .4406769
       EFI |  -.7171632   .4069815    -1.76   0.091    -1.557132   .1228054
     _cons |   64.45491   31.04903     2.08   0.049    .3728712    128.537
```

Secondly, I used the existence of a European identity and the composite Economic Freedom index as independent variables. Surprisingly the Existence of a European identity is not significantly related to the continuous variable FEL. Only when we use the binary variable EON like above is it possible to detect a difference. On the contrary, EFI has a negative influence significant at the 10% level. Voters that enjoy a higher degree of economic freedom might fear that Europeanization will impose more regulation and bureaucracy.

```
reg FEL  TEC EEI ICC

    Source |       SS        df        MS              Number of obs =      27
-----------+----------------------------------         F(  3,   23) =     4.50
     Model |  518.107782       3   172.702594          Prob > F      =   0.0126
  Residual |  882.410737      23   38.3656842          R-squared     =   0.3699
-----------+----------------------------------         Adj R-squared =   0.2878
     Total |  1400.51852      26   53.8660969          Root MSE      =    6.194


       FEL |      Coef.   Std. Err.      t    P>|t|     [95% Conf. Interval]
-----------+----------------------------------------------------------------
       TEC |    .442743   .1582239     2.80   0.010    .1154319    .7700541
       EEI |  -.1501734   .1494916    -1.00   0.326    -.4594204   .1590737
       ICC |  -.2408756   .1099867    -2.19   0.039    -.4684004  -.0133508
     _cons |   28.04445   13.2706      2.11   0.046    .5921136    55.49678
```

I found the most interesting and significant results when I added TEC and ICC. I included EEI as a control variable because it thought that it might partly explain the effect of TEC. However, the results seem unambiguous. The most important predictor for the desirability of European action is the trust that people put in the European commission. This is not surprising; however, the public choice analysis has shown that even honest and altruistic bureaucrats might do more evil than good. Because voters have problems to detect the advantages of decentralization, their trust might lead them to wrong assumptions.

The other important factor is ICC. The ICC score was composed of two questions: "Foreign ownership of companies in your country is rare, limited to minority stakes and often prohibited in key sectors (= 1) or prevalent and encouraged (= 7)"; and "In your country, rules governing foreign direct investment are damaging and discourage foreign direct investment (= 1) or beneficial and encourage foreign direct investment (= 7)." People in countries that are more open to foreign capital are less supportive of European action. They might fear that Europeanization will decrease this openness through more bureaucracy and their country could lose its competitive advantage.

A close look at the relationship between FEL and ICC reveals that there are several outliers. Spain (ES) and Poland (PL) have a financial market that is protected from foreign competition through strong controls. These countries strongly favor the EU level. On the other hand, the Netherlands (NL), the United Kingdom (UK) and Ireland (IE) have very open capital markets and strongly oppose European level for financial measures. The other countries could be regarded as "stuck-in-the-middle" from a management point of view, they would not loose or gain much in this area.

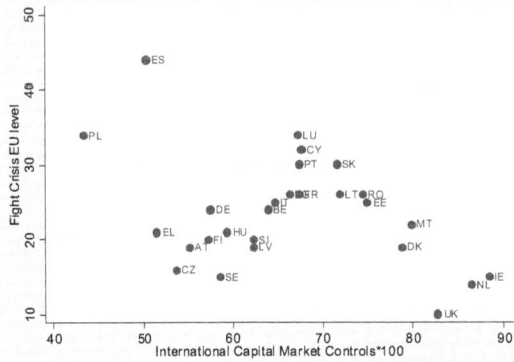

If we just look at the relationship between FEL and TEC again, the relationship seems obvious.

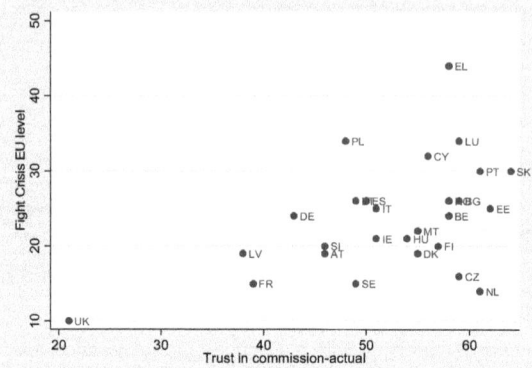

It is not surprising that the UK is the most skeptical country. However, it is more revealing to pick some other countries. Greece (EL) support for European action is unsurprisingly even stronger than their trust in the Commission would have suggested. The Netherlands (NL), Sweden (SE), and the Czech Republic (CZ) on the other hand have trust in the EC, but do nonetheless over-proportionally oppose more Europeanization.

Supervision over transparency

Regarding the preference for supervision over transparency, it is not possible to derive clear relationships with this limited dataset. Regressing on the binary variable did not yield significant estimates for any meaningful explanatory variable.

```
. logit  SOT TEC SML

Iteration 0:   log likelihood = -17.797118
Iteration 1:   log likelihood = -17.282867
Iteration 2:   log likelihood = -17.281304
Iteration 3:   log likelihood = -17.281304

Logistic regression                               Number of obs   =        27
                                                  LR chi2(2)      =      1.03
                                                  Prob > chi2     =    0.5970
Log likelihood = -17.281304                       Pseudo R2       =    0.0290

------------------------------------------------------------------------------
         SOT |     Coef.   Std. Err.      z    P>|z|     [95% Conf. Interval]
-------------+----------------------------------------------------------------
         TEC |  -.0203832   .0462605    -0.44   0.659    -.1110521    .0702856
         SML |  -.0440768    .04466     -0.99   0.324    -.1316087    .0434551
       _cons |   4.199213   4.123945     1.02   0.309    -3.883571     12.282
------------------------------------------------------------------------------


. logit  SOT TEC EFI

Iteration 0:   log likelihood = -17.797118
Iteration 1:   log likelihood = -17.416333
Iteration 2:   log likelihood = -17.415203
Iteration 3:   log likelihood = -17.415203

Logistic regression                               Number of obs   =        27
                                                  LR chi2(2)      =      0.76
                                                  Prob > chi2     =    0.6826
Log likelihood = -17.415203                       Pseudo R2       =    0.0215

------------------------------------------------------------------------------
         SOT |     Coef.   Std. Err.      z    P>|z|     [95% Conf. Interval]
-------------+----------------------------------------------------------------
         TEC |  -.0155398   .0451707    -0.34   0.731    -.1040728    .0729932
         EFI |  -.108866    .1284221    -0.85   0.397    -.3605687    .1428367
       _cons |   9.362104   10.36008     0.90   0.366    -10.94327    29.66748
------------------------------------------------------------------------------
```

People seem to be split about the decision, which reform to prefer. There is no clear pattern in countries that do prefer more regulation and supervision. It is likely that voters have faith in more supervision, regardless of their origin. Even SML, the feeling that the state interferes too much in individual lives is not significantly negatively related to SOT. It seems like people in the member states have unique preferences about state intervention in their lives.

Another interesting point is that feeling as a European is more a cultural issue than related to state interference and supervision. An important factor seems to be the geographic location. The four countries with the lowest European identity Bulgaria (BG), Cyprus (CY), Lithuania (LV) and the UK are all situated on the periphery of the EU. Obviously, this graph cannot completely clarify this issue. Hence, it is useful to have a look at another relationship to further analyze preferences.

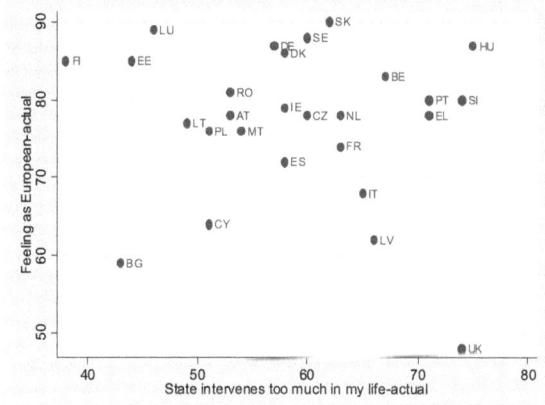

It can be seen that the relationship between actual economic freedom and the subjective feelings that SML expresses is not clear. There are countries like Bulgaria (BG) that have a low EFI, but voters do not experience state intervention as too high. The result of Slovenia (SI) is more in line with common sense. However, people in the UK are amidst the ones to enjoy the highest EFI, but experience SML as too high. In my view this is a beautiful example how preferences in the EU differ, and that the same circumstances are judged differently by people with a different cultural background. Hence, a level of regulation that people in Luxemburg (LU) and Finland would accept, could be experienced as an unwelcome intrusion into their personal freedom.

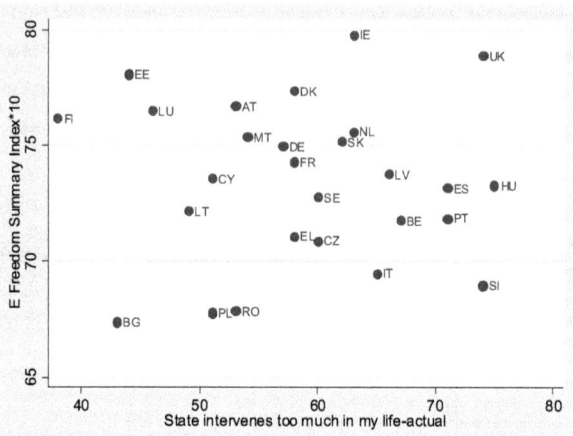